# HIP TO BEAD

## 32
## Contemporary
## Projects
## for Today's Beader

*Katie Hacker*

INTERWEAVE PRESS
www.interweave.com

## ACKNOWLEDGMENTS

This book is dedicated, as always, to my husband, Craig, and our families. I'm grateful for their constant support and encouragement. ■ I would also like to thank the team at Interweave Press for contributing their considerable talents, time, and energy to this book. ■ Grateful thanks to all of the companies who generously provided beads and stringing materials. ■ Special thanks to my fellow artist-entrepreneurs and Society of Creative Designers members, especially: Debba Haupert, Lisa Galvin, Margot Potter, and Mary Lynn Maloney for their advice and insights into the writing process. ■ Thanks also to Kate Carter for knitting and felting the lovely aqua handbag and to Fernando Dasilva for collaborating on the glamorous ear-threader idea. Grateful thanks to all of the companies who generously provided beading supplies for use in this book: Beadalon; Blue Moon Beads; Fire Mountain Gems and Beads; Halcraft USA, Inc.; JHB International; Kristal Wick Creations; Lillypilly Designs; Paula Radke Dichroic Glass Beads; Pure Allure; Rio Grande; Swarovski North America, Ltd.; Thunderbird Supply Company; and Toho Co., Ltd.

Editor: Christine Townsend
Technical Editor: Bonnie Brooks
Art Director: Paulette Livers
Series Designer: Bren Frisch
Production: Pauline Brown
Photography: Joe Coca
Illustration: Ann Swanson
Photo Styling: Ann Swanson
Proofreader and Indexer: Nancy Arndt

Interweave Press LLC
201 East Fourth Street
Loveland, Colorado 80537-5655 USA
www.interweave.com

Printed and bound in China through Asia Pacific.

Library of Congress Cataloging-in-Publication Data

Hacker, Katie.
  Hip to bead : 32 contemporary designs for beaders / Katie Hacker, author.
    p. cm.
  ISBN 1-931499-95-0
  1. Beadwork. 2. Jewelry making. I. Title.
  TT860.H33 2006
  745.594'2--dc22
                          2005022359

10 9 8 7 6 5 4 3 2 1

# ■ CONTENTS

**1** Introduction
**2** Basics
    Beads,   3
    Components,   5
    Stringing Materials,   7
    Tools,   8

**PROJECTS**
**Easy Assembly**
**12** Chic Antique Button Bracelet
**14** Stylish Scrapbook
**16** Found Object Charm Bracelet

**Super Stringing**
**20** Chunky Nugget Necklace
**22** Double Trouble Choker
**24** Follow Your Heart Faux Lariat
**26** Twice as Nice Necklace
**30** Time to Bead Watch
**32** Fit-for-a-Queen Bracelet
**35** Great Lengths Necklace
    and Bracelet
**38** Luscious Lariat
**42** In Vogue Purse

**Getting Wired**
**46** Quick and Easy Earrings
**48** Sparkly Beaded Barrettes
**50** Rock 'N Roll Cuff
**52** Y Not? Necklace
**54** Cha-Cha Bracelet
**56** Glamour Girl Chandeliers
**57** Clever Candle Wrap
**58** Mod Millefiori Necklace

**Knotty But Nice**
**62** World Beat Choker
**64** Center Stage Opera Necklace
**66** Knock-Out Knotted Necklace
**68** Knotty Hemp Belt

**Rich Stitches**
**72** Trendy Tank Top
**74** Retro Beaded Journal
**76** Aloha Flower Frame
**78** Funky Felted Purse

**Woven Wonders**
**82** Bejeweled Crystal Bracelet
**84** Oceanside Bling Necklace
**86** Creative Cause Bracelet
**88** Righteous Right-Angle Weave Bracelet

**90** Suppliers
**91** Index

## TECHNIQUES AND TIPS

**15** Choosing the Right Adhesive

**17** Charm Bracelet Tips

**21** Combining Colors

**23** Working with Memory Wire

**25** Personalizing Your Designs

**28** Using Crimps to Attach a Clasp

**31** Helpful Hints for Making Watches

**34** All About Art Glass

**37** Standard Jewelry Lengths

**41** Common Beading Patterns

**47** Making Wire Loops

**53** Hill Tribe Silver

**59** Making Bead Links

**61** Knotting Between Beads

**65** Using Chain

**70** Tying Square Knots

**77** Backstitch with Beads

**78** Blanket Stitch with Beads

**85** Right-Angle Weave

**87** Tubular Peyote Stitch

# INTRODUCTION

Ever since I made my first friendship bracelet, I've been in love with handmade jewelry. During high school, I experimented with simple earrings and necklaces and, while in college, I got interested in hemp jewelry and macramé. I love the way a piece of jewelry can complete your whole outfit. Don't you? ■ Beads come in such a wide variety of shapes, forms, and colors and have such an interesting cultural and historical significance that they're a veritable treasure trove for the imagination. Just collecting beads can be a pleasure in itself, but this book will give you ideas for how to turn beads into beautiful, functional jewelry, gifts, and accessories. ■ This is a step-by-step idea book that features projects that you can make in an evening or a weekend. The Basics section includes general information about beads, components, stringing materials, and tools, and it's the perfect place to start if you're a beginner or just need a good reference. ■ No matter what your skill level is, you're sure to discover a project in the following pages that sparks your imagination. The projects cover basic assembly, stringing, knotting, wirework, bead embroidery, and bead weaving, and they are divided into chapters based on technique. The easier projects at the beginning lead to more complex projects toward the end. Be sure to check out the sidebars and variations for additional information, ideas, and tips. ■ As you create your own hip versions of these projects, you'll find that it's refreshing to make something practical, beautiful, and beaded. There's no better feeling than being able to say "I made it myself!"

# BASICS

## SUPPLIES AND TIPS
## TO HELP YOU GET STARTED

The secret to making your own designer jewelry
and beaded gifts is using beautiful beads, classy
components, and durable stringing materials
and tools. In this section, you'll find descriptions
of everything you'll need to make your own
hip creations.

## ■ BEADS

Beads are available in an incredible variety of colors, shapes, sizes, and materials. They come in every price range, too, so it's easy to find beads that fit your vision and your budget. Here's a sampling of the beads used in this book, along with tips and ideas for how to use them.

**Base metal silver beads** are made of nonprecious metals such as aluminum, brass, copper, and nickel. They're more economical than sterling silver beads but cannot be polished to remove tarnish.

**Bugle beads** are glass beads made of cut glass cane. Bugle beads tend to have very sharp edges, so use them with durable beading thread or beading wire.

**Crystal beads** are mainly made in Austria. These leaded glass beads add sparkle to beaded designs and are available in a variety of shapes (round, bicone, cube, briolette). Their sharp edges can cause abrasion, so string them on durable beading wire.

**Crystal pearls** are leaded glass beads with a pearl finish. Their heft is similar to cultured pearls without the price tag.

**Dichroic glass beads** are made of layers of sparkly multicolored glass. They tend to be heavy, so use them with stringing materials appropriate for their weight.

**Fire-polished beads** are typically less expensive and less abrasive than crystal beads and add a fair amount of sparkle to beaded designs. A surface finish called aurora borealis (AB) is sometimes added to create a rainbowlike effect.

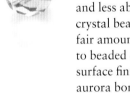

**Freshwater pearls** are much less expensive than cultured pearls and add a lustrous quality to beaded designs. Hole size is often an issue, so keep a bead reamer (see page 9) handy for enlarging them.

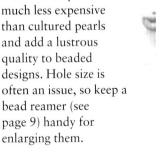

**Gemstone beads** come in a wide variety of shapes, sizes, and materials, from translucent amethyst to opaque jet. Good quality gemstones have evenly drilled holes that are perfectly centered on the stone. Use a bead reamer to file abrasive or uneven bead holes.

**Handpainted silk beads** are tube shapes made of stiffened silk. When you use thin stringing material, place a smaller bead inside the hole to reduce the size of the opening.

**Lampworked beads** (including borosilicate) are handmade by artists worldwide. They tend to be heavy, so use them with stringing materials appropriate for their weight.

**Millefiori beads** were originally made in Italy; the name translates as "a thousand flowers." They typically feature brightly colored mosaics of tiny flowers. Inexpensive versions are now made in China.

**Sequins** are flat disks with a hole in the center. They make a good base for seed beads stitched to fabric. Layer a seed bead on top of a sequin, then pass back through the sequin to hold it in place.

**Size 6°° seed beads** are also called pony beads. They're similar to size 11° seed beads but larger. Use them as spacers or in woven projects.

**Size 11° seed beads** are available in round or cylindrical shapes. Round seed beads make nice beaded strands, while cylindrical seed beads are perfect for weaving. Use them with beading thread for the softest, most flexible drape or with beading wire for more durability.

**Sterling silver beads** must be made of at least 92.5 percent pure silver to be sold as sterling silver. Sterling components typically have a stamp that says "925" to identify them as sterling silver, but beads typically do not. Handmade sterling beads from Bali and Thailand have distinctive designs and are widely copied in base metal versions. Sterling is prone to tarnish, so store it in an airtight container.

## ■ COMPONENTS

Components can often make the difference between a beautiful handmade and a boring homemade piece of jewelry. They're available in a wide variety of styles and metals. When you choose metals, try to match the value of the components to the value of the beads. If you're stringing expensive gemstones, don't use cheap base metal components.

**Chain** is often used as a design element and comes in a wide variety of styles.

**End connectors** have a loop on one side and multiple loops on the other side. They're used to attach multiple strands to one clasp or as decorative elements in a design.

**Crimp beads** look like seed beads, but they are actually tiny metal beads that flatten when they're squeezed with pliers. Use them to hold beaded sections in place on a wire.

**Crimp ends** fasten easily to beading wire. Place the wire inside the crimp end, then use chain-nose piers or a crimping tool to squeeze the sides together.

**Crimp tubes** are cylindrical metal beads that attach clasps to beaded designs. Use a crimping tool to crimp them.

A **duet clasp** has two identical parts that fit together at the gap. It's similar to a toggle clasp, but it doesn't need extra length for the parts to fit together.

**Ear wires** are used to make dangly pierced earrings. The fishhook style is basically a curved wire that's open on the back. The leverback style clips in the back to prevent the earring from falling out of the ear.

**Eye pins** are pieces of thin wire with a premade loop on the end. Use them as connectors between beads or beaded head pins.

**French wire** is a tiny coil of wire that's used to protect silk cord from the abrasion of the clasp.

**Gemstone links** make decorative dangles; they can also be used to connect two parts of a design.

**Head pins** are thin pieces of wire with a nail head or a decorative element on the end that prevents beads from sliding off. Use them to make dangles.

**Jump rings** are made of a single loop and should be opened by turning the ends laterally rather than by pulling them directly apart.

A **lobster clasp** is a classic type of clasp that's easy to open and close. Clasp to a jump ring or split ring to fasten it.

**S-hooks** fasten to jump rings to hold the ends of a necklace together. It isn't necessary to open and close an S-hook each time you wear a necklace. In fact, doing so will quickly wear out the clasp. For best results, open one side of the S-hook just enough to slide on the jump ring and leave it open. The necklace will still be secure.

**Sliders** are metal components with two holes on each end. They add a designer look to double-strand designs.

**Split rings** are made of two connected loops like a key ring and are more secure than ordinary jump rings.

A **toggle clasp** is made up of a ring and bar that fit together. Be sure the beads at the end of a design do not prevent the bar from fitting through the ring.

## ■ STRINGING MATERIALS

To make durable jewelry and beaded gifts, it's important to choose the right foundation. Each type of stringing material has specific qualities, and the trick is deciding which is best for your design. Here's a sampling of stringing materials and suggestions for how to use them.

**Beading thread** is specially made to resist abrasion. In comparing thread width to bead hole size to choose the diameter, keep in mind that some projects call for the thread to pass more than once through the beads.

**Beading wire** is made from stranded threads of fine stainless steel wire which makes it as strong as steel but as soft as thread. The number of threads determines the wire's flexibility. Choose the diameter that works best with the bead hole size, unless a particular size is specified in the instructions.

**Craft wire** is available in a variety of colors and is typically inexpensive. Use it for home décor and inexpensive jewelry projects.

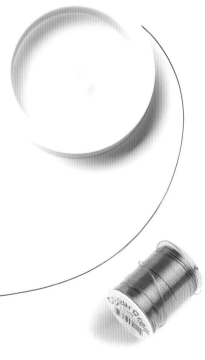

**Faux suede cord** is softer than genuine suede and tends to lie flatter in a beaded design. It's available in an array of colors and can be knotted. Use metal cord ends to attach a clasp.

**Hemp cord** is a natural twine commonly used for macramé projects. Good quality hemp has consistent diameter. Hemp softens with wear.

**Memory wire** is stainless steel wire that keeps its shape. It's available in preformed necklace, bracelet, and ring sizes. Use only shears that are specially made to cut hardened wire because memory wire will ruin ordinary wire cutters.

## Silk thread and cord

come in a variety of colors and diameters. Choose the diameter that works best with the bead hole size. This fiber is typically sold on the card with a needle attached. Stretch out any creases before knotting.

**Sterling wire** is typically used for wire wrapping and is available in a variety of diameters. The projects in this book use half-hard wire.

## ■ TOOLS

The number of grades of tools makes it easy to find those that fit your budget. Look for tools that are specially made for beading and buy the best quality that you can afford. Here are the tools used in this book and tips for how to use them.

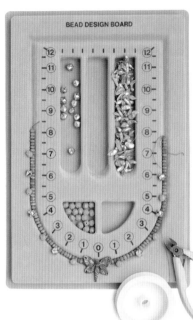

## Bead boards

make it easy to measure a design as you work and to see what designs will look like before you string them. A measuring tape may also come in handy for use with a bead board.

## Sharp beading needles

are very fine needles that fit through the tiniest of beads when threaded. For easy threading, use a needle threader or hold the thread still and place the needle eye onto it.

**Round-nose pliers** have tapered round jaws that are used to make loops.

**Wire cutters** have sharp jaws that are used to cut beading wire, head pins, eye pins, and other soft wire. Wire cutters come in a variety of styles. For a close cut on beading wire or wire head pins and eye pins, use cutters with diagonal blades. Do not use them to cut memory wire.

**Crimping tools** are used to squeeze and secure crimp beads or tubes on beading wire. (see page 5)

**Chain-nose pliers** are a jewelry maker's version of needle-nose pliers. They have tapered half-round jaws that are smooth inside. Use them to open and close jump rings and for wire wrapping.

**Beading awls** are used for placing knots precisely between beads. Knotting tools are similar, but make faster, more consistent knots. (see page 61)

knotting tool

beading awl

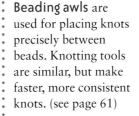

**Bead reamers** are round files that fit inside bead holes. Use them to smooth abrasive edges or to enlarge holes. Place the tip inside the bead hole and twist the reamer from side to side.

**Memory-wire shears** are specially made for cutting hardened wire that will damage ordinary wire cutters.

**Split-ring pliers** have a pointed end that fits down between the rings of a split ring to open it. Use split-ring pliers instead of your fingernails to separate rings.

# EASY ASSEMBLY

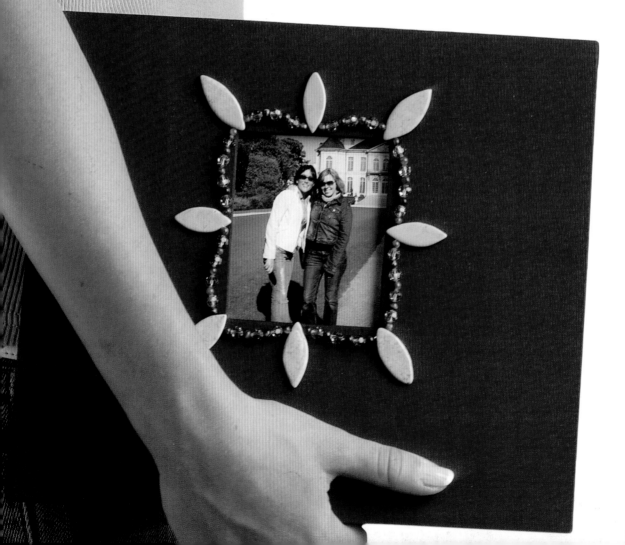

# EASY ASSEMBLY

So you've heard that it's easy to make your own jewelry and beaded gifts, but you're not too sure where to begin. ■ The projects in this chapter will give you a gentle introduction to working with beads. ■ Once you get started, there will be no stopping you!

## CHIC ANTIQUE BUTTON
# BRACELET

This fun bracelet is a perfect way to use those cool old buttons that you've collected from yard sales or grandma's button box. If you don't have a vintage stash, hit your local fabric store and look for buttons with a retro vibe.

*It's a modern twist on an old favorite...*

**Step 1.** Choose enough buttons to cover the connectors on the bracelet. Use four or five buttons that have texture (shamrock, Route 66, question mark, swirl) to add interest. Choose equal numbers of silver and brightly colored buttons with and without shanks.

**Step 2.** For any buttons without shanks, use smaller buttons or flat-back crystals to cover the holes.

**Step 3.** Arrange the buttons in the order that you're going to attach them to the bracelet. The sample shows two silver buttons near the center, but the rest are alternating bright and silver. Adjust the order of the buttons until you're happy with the design.

## ■ MATERIALS

6 brightly colored or pearl
12–15mm buttons

6 silver 12–15mm textured
buttons

2–3 silver or black 4–8mm
flat-back crystals

Silver linked ring-and-
connector bracelet

## ■ TOOLS

Epoxy
Heavy-duty wire cutters
Fine metal file
Popsicle stick

## ■ FINISHED SIZE

7½" (19 cm) (length of
purchased bracelet)

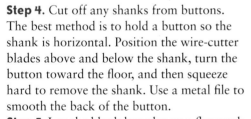

**Step 4.** Cut off any shanks from buttons.
The best method is to hold a button so the
shank is horizontal. Position the wire-cutter
blades above and below the shank, turn the
button toward the floor, and then squeeze
hard to remove the shank. Use a metal file to
smooth the back of the button.

**Step 5.** Lay the blank bracelet on a flat work
surface with the connectors facing up. Use a
popsicle stick to spread a thin layer of epoxy
onto the back of each button and attach
them one at a time to the bracelet.

**Step 6.** While the epoxy is still wet, press a
smaller button or rhinestone over the holes
on any buttons without shanks. Let the
epoxy dry overnight.

## ■ VARIATION

String a collection of antique buttons
with shanks onto beading wire for a
no-glue version of the button bracelet.
In this example, mixed metallic colors
combine with sparkly rhinestones to
create a classy vintage assemblage.
Choose buttons with narrow shanks
so they'll fit closely together on
the bracelet, and be sure to use the
thickest beading wire that will fit
through the shanks. After all the
buttons are strung, just add a toggle
clasp. (see page 6)

# SCRAPBOOK

It takes only a few beads and some wire to make a personalized scrapbook that's as unique as the photos inside. This project is a great gift—but be sure to make one for yourself, too!

*Raise the glam factor on a plain Jane scrapbook.*

## ■ MATERIALS

- Purple scrapbook with 2¾ x 3¼" (7 x 8.5 cm) photo opening
- 8 chalk turquoise 30mm leaf beads
- 28 lavender 6mm faceted round crystal beads
- 36 tiger's eye 4mm round beads
- 14" (35.5 cm) of 26-gauge gold craft wire
- Industrial strength glue
- Adhesive tape

## ■ TOOLS

- Chain-nose pliers
- Wire cutters

## ■ FINISHED SIZE

- 8¾ x 10¼" (22 x 26 cm) or size of scrapbook you choose

**Step 1.** Place a piece of adhesive tape 1" from the wire end to prevent beads from sliding off.

**Step 2.** Pass the wire end through a tiger's eye bead and a crystal bead.

**Step 3.** Repeat Step 2 two more times, then pass the wire end through a tiger's eye bead and a leaf bead.

**Step 4.** Repeat Step 2 four times, then pass the wire end through a tiger's eye bead and a leaf bead.

**Step 5.** Repeat Steps 2–4 to string all the beads onto the wire.

**Step 6.** Place the wire ends through opposite ends of the last bead.

**Step 7.** Wrap the wire ends in a tight coil around the wire between the last beads.

**Step 8.** Use wire cutters to cut off any extra wire.

**Step 9.** Place the beaded wire over the picture opening. Hold the leaves down and push the edges in to create the scalloped effect.

**Step 10.** Glue the leaves to the album. If necessary, tape the leaves in place until the glue dries.

## CHOOSING THE RIGHT ADHESIVE

There are so many glues on the market that it can be tricky to know which one to use. Experience is the best teacher, so play with as many different adhesives as you can. You'll develop your own preferences, but here are some guidelines:

■ **Epoxy:** This is two-step glue, which means you have to mix two parts together. It makes a permanent bond. Use it to glue flat beads to flat surfaces or to attach end caps to wire or cord ends. Epoxy takes a long time to dry, but it's worth the wait.

■ **Fabric glue:** This type of adhesive creates a strong, flexible bond on porous surfaces. Choose thick glue that won't soak through, like Fabri-Tac. Use it to adhere beaded ribbon or leather to a fabric surface.

■ **Industrial strength glue:** Use this adhesive when you need thick glue that will make a strong bond. It's handy for gluing beads onto a variety of nonporous surfaces. Common brands are E6000 and Glass, Metal & More.

■ **Jeweler's cement:** Most commonly used when a flexible bond is called for, jeweler's cement has a fine tip applicator that makes it easy to apply. Use it to glue the ends of woven or knotted projects. Look for G-S Hypo Cement or Dazzle-Tac.

# FOUND OBJECT CHARM
# BRACELET

Charm bracelets are timeless pieces of jewelry that manage to be trendy, classy, and fun all at once. Use found objects to create your own hip take on a classic or to create clever personalized gifts.

*. . . look for playful game pieces and hip hardware . . .*

## ■ MATERIALS

- Game pieces and dice
- Interesting washers or other hardware with holes
- Small keys and padlocks
- Blank brass charms
- Jump rings in assorted sizes
- Length of 16-gauge silver wire
- Length of sterling silver chain
- 2 sterling silver 6mm split rings
- Sterling silver toggle clasp

## ■ TOOLS

- Chain-nose pliers
- Wire cutters
- Split-ring pliers
- Drill with $1/16$" bit
- Epoxy

## ■ FINISHED SIZE

- Measure wrist and add $1/2$" (1.3 cm)

**Step 1.** Choose a clasp and use split-ring pliers to attach a split ring to each part of the clasp.

**Step 2.** Measure the clasp/split ring combination and subtract it from the total desired length of the bracelet.

**Step 3.** Cut the sterling chain to the proper length and use a split ring to attach half of the clasp to each end.

**Step 4.** Flat game disks: glue a disk inside a plain brass charm. Cover it with epoxy or cut a transparent dimensional sticker to fit inside the charm.

**Step 5.** Washers or other hardware with holes: use jump rings to attach them to the bracelet singly or together for a layered look.

**Step 6.** Dice: drill a hole in one side. Use 16-gauge wire to make a basic loop and glue the wire end inside the hole.

**Step 7.** Game tiles: drill a hole through the top center of a small tile. For larger tiles, drill through the corner so the tile hangs at an angle on the bracelet.

**Step 8.** Use jump rings to attach each charm to the bracelet.

## CHARM BRACELET TIPS

■ **Even if you haven't been collecting charms since you were born,** you can still put together a cool charm bracelet that reflects your personality. Purchase charms for places you've been, favorite hobbies, or children's birthstones.

■ **Don't be afraid to add charms with a sense of humor.** Look for funny vintage charms or use charms that just make you smile. I added an "I love Monster Trucks" charm to a bracelet for my sister because we once drove a monster truck, and it was a totally fun (and funny) experience.

■ **Use alphabet charms to spell a** person's name or a phrase like "Hip to Bead."

■ **Look at the overall composition.** If you've used lots of silver charms, add some color with crystal beads.

■ **Most charms come with a jump ring** attached. Split rings are a safer choice for securing unique or beloved charms, and they don't take much more time to attach. Use split-ring pliers to facilitate opening.

■ **If your bracelet features absolutely irreplaceable charms,** solder the rings closed or ask a jeweler to do the soldering for you.

■ **Increase the versatility** of a charm bracelet by adding a long strip of suede lacing with attached clasp ends that work with the bracelet clasp. Voilà! Instant necklace.

■ **Charm bracelets make great gifts.** Consider the following themes: Travel, Mom-to-Be, Lucky Charms, Wedding Day, or Girly Girl.

# SUPER STRINGING

**STRINGING IS ONE OF THE MOST** basic beading techniques and it's used to make all kinds of projects, from simple single-strand creations to elaborate multistrand extravaganzas. ■ This chapter will give you lots of ideas for creating your own hip designs, so let's get started!

# CHUNKY NUGGET
# NECKLACE

This is the easiest necklace to make on the planet, and its statement is strong. Combine bright, eye-catching colors in a repeating pattern with the world's simplest clasp. Then sit back and wait for the compliments.

*This bold choker is the easiest necklace ever.*

**Step 1.** Place one side of the clasp on the end of the beading wire.
**Step 2.** Use chain-nose pliers or the outer jaws of the crimping tool to squeeze the sides of the clasp together.
**Step 3.** Pull gently to make sure the clasp is attached.
**Step 4.** String 1 rondelle, 1 crystal, 1 rondelle, and 1 nugget on the wire. Repeat this step twelve more times.
**Step 5.** String 1 rondelle, 1 crystal, 1 rondelle, and follow Step 2 to attach the other side of the clasp.

## ■ MATERIALS

- 13 chalk turquoise 25mm nuggets
- 14 tanzanite 8mm crystal cube beads
- 28 Hill tribe silver 6mm rondelle beads

Silver S-hook EZ crimp clasp
16" length of .024" diameter beading wire

## ■ TOOLS

Chain-nose pliers or crimping tool
Wire cutters

## ■ FINISHED SIZE

16½" (42 cm)

## COMBINING COLORS

A color wheel is a great way to come up with color combinations. You can also look at fashion magazines or paint chips for color inspiration. It's easier to combine two colors than three, so start small. Keep in mind that shape, texture, and luster all affect how bead colors come together. Stretch out of your comfort zone by trying some of the following combinations. You may be surprised by the results!

**Hip two-color combinations:**
- ■ Red jasper and jet (red and black)
- ■ Sodalite and carnelian (dark blue and orange)
- ■ Rose quartz and citrine (pink and light yellow)
- ■ Amethyst and aventurine (purple and green)
- ■ Tiger's eye and turquoise (striated brown and aqua)

**Hip three-color combinations:**
- ■ Lemon chrysoprase, carnelian, and peridot (yellow, orange, and green)
- ■ Garnet, amethyst, and citrine (red, purple, and yellow)
- ■ Peridot, iolite, and amethyst (green, blue, and purple)
- ■ Garnet, peridot, and rose quartz (red, green, and pink)

## DOUBLE TROUBLE
# CHOKER

Use turquoise chips and tiny crystal beads to make this cool wraparound choker. Since it's made with memory wire, you don't need a clasp to connect the ends. Black rubber tubing adds a chic look and hides the wire between the beads.

*Make this cool wraparound choker.*

■ **VARIATION**

The best feature of using black rubber tubing to cover memory wire is achieving the look of cord without using large-hole beads. In this variation, the lampworked, Bali silver, and crystal beads are strung directly onto the wire. Lengths of tubing cover the wire on both sides. Memory wire end caps are glued onto the wire to cover the ends.

## ■ MATERIALS

69 turquoise chips
26 clear 3mm faceted round
    crystal beads
14" length of 1.7mm diameter
    black rubber tubing

4 silver 1" (2.5 cm) head pins
2 continuous loops of
    necklace-size memory wire

## ■ TOOLS

Round-nose pliers
Chain-nose pliers
Wire cutters
Scissors

## ■ FINISHED SIZE

One size fits all

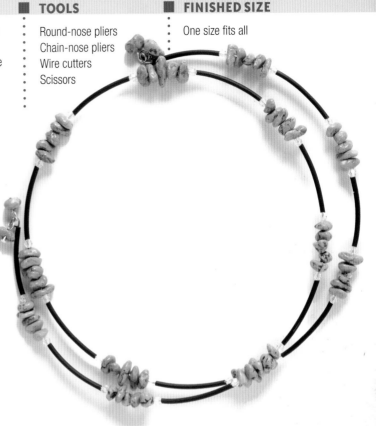

**Step 1.** Use scissors to cut the rubber tubing into fourteen 1" (2.5 cm) lengths.

**Step 2.** Use round-nose pliers to make a loop on one end of the memory wire. (see page 47)

**Step 3.** String a length of rubber tubing, 1 crystal, 5 chips, and 1 crystal. Repeat this step twelve more times.

**Step 4.** String a length of rubber tubing and make a loop at the end of the wire.

**Step 5.** String a chip onto each head pin. Make a basic loop above each chip.

**Step 6.** Attach 2 chips to the loop on each end of the necklace.

## WORKING WITH MEMORY WIRE

■ **Memory wire is tempered wire that** remembers its shape and retains its coiled form. It's basically one size fits all and comes in preformed necklace, bracelet, and ring sizes. You don't need a clasp to connect the ends because they automatically stay in place on your neck, wrist, or finger.

■ **To cut loops of memory wire,** use shears that are made especially for hardened wire. Do not use ordinary wire cutters because the memory wire will cut into the blades and ruin them.

■ **When you place beads on the wire,** it's important to keep the wire in its natural shape. Don't pull the wire straight, or the ends may bounce back and the beads will fly off.

■ **When you finish the ends with a basic loop,** try bending the wire against the natural curve. Sometimes this is easier to do than forcing it to bend into the curve.

■ **Use epoxy or cyanoacrylic glue to glue end caps onto the wire ends.** Place a drop of glue on the end of the wire and press an end cap on. String a few beads, then spot-glue the last few beads together to help hold the end cap in place.

# FOLLOW YOUR
## HEART FAUX
# LARIAT

Thread faux suede cord through a large focal bead,

then add a few dangling beads and charms. The piece

looks like a lariat, but fastens like a regular necklace.

What could be more simple and chic?

**Step 1.** Use scissors to cut the suede cord into one
12½" (31.5 cm) length and one 13½" (34.5 cm) length.
**Step 2.** Tie an overhand knot ½" (1.3 cm) from one end
of each length of suede.
**Step 3.** String one 6mm silver bead, 1 tan tube, and the
dragonfly onto the 12½" (31.5 cm) length.
**Step 4.** String the spiral bead, one 6mm bead, 1 purple tube,
and 1 6mm silver bead onto the 13½" (34.5 cm) length.
**Step 5.** Hold the other end of the suede cords together
and string the winged heart bead.
**Step 6.** Place a C-crimp cord end on the end of each suede
length. Use chain-nose pliers to gently close the crimp.
**Step 7.** Use a jump ring to attach the clasp to one end and
the extension chain to the other end.
**Step 8.** String 1 crystal onto a head pin. Make a basic
loop, but leave the loop open. Attach it to the end of the
extension chain for a sweet little finishing touch.

## ■ MATERIALS

- Silver 10mm winged heart bead
- 2 painted silk 12mm tube beads: tan, purple
- Hill tribe silver 22mm dragonfly bead
- Hill tribe silver 12mm spiral bead
- 3 silver 6mm round large-hole beads
- Olivine 4mm bicone crystal bead
- 26" (66 cm) of green faux suede cord
- 2 silver C-crimp cord ends
- 2 silver 5mm jump rings
- Silver lobster clasp
- Silver extension chain
- Silver 1" (2.5 cm) head pin

## ■ TOOLS

- Chain-nose pliers
- Wire cutters
- Scissors

## ■ FINISHED SIZE

16–18" (40.5–45.5 cm)

### PERSONALIZING YOUR DESIGNS

Make designs more meaningful by adding charms or beads that have special significance to you or the recipient. These personal talismans make the piece uniquely individual; they also infuse your own creative energy into the design. Most symbols have many meanings, but here are a few common ones to get you started:

**Dragonfly:** Regeneration
**Spiral:** Interconnectedness
**Heart:** Love
**Wings:** Freedom
**Star:** Dream
**Bear:** Protection
**Labyrinth:** Journey
**Turtle:** Longevity
**Hand:** Creativity
**Flower:** Beauty

# TWICE AS NICE
# NECKLACE

Who says less is more? The layered look is
in! This necklace looks like you're cleverly
wearing two coordinating necklaces,
but it's actually just one double-strand
design. Combine gorgeous gemstones
with handmade silver beads to make two
delicious strands.

## ■ MATERIALS

- Hill tribe silver 25mm pendant
- 6 Hill tribe silver 8mm eye charms
- 4 Hill tribe silver 10mm spiral charms
- 44 carnelian 6mm round beads
- 18 garnet 6mm faceted buttons
- 10 aventurine 6mm buttons
- 16 Hill tribe silver 5mm beads
- 2 Hill tribe silver 6mm beads
- 5 Hill tribe silver 8mm beads
- 48 sterling silver chips
- 26 green 6° seed beads
- 160 silver 11° seed beads
- Sterling silver S-hook clasp
- 2 sterling silver soldered jump rings
- 4 sterling silver crimp tubes
- 39" (99 cm) of beading wire

## ■ TOOLS

- Wire cutters
- Crimping tool

## ■ FINISHED SIZE

- 16½" (42 cm) shorter strand

**Step 1.** Use wire cutters to cut the beading wire into two lengths: 18½" (47 cm) and 20½" (52 cm)

**Step 2.** Use a crimp tube to attach a jump ring to one end of the 18½" (47 cm) length. (See page 28)

**Step 3.** String the following beads onto the wire: one 6°, 1 carnelian, one 8mm silver, 1 carnelian, one 6°.

**Step 4.** String 20 silver seed beads, one 5mm silver bead, 1 garnet button, one 5mm silver bead, and 20 silver seed beads.

**Step 5.** Alternate Steps 3–4 four times as shown, then repeat Step 3.

**Step 6.** Use a crimp tube to attach the wire end to the other jump ring. Use wire cutters to cut off any extra wire.

**Step 7.** Use a crimp tube to attach the 20½" (52 cm) length of wire to the first jump ring.

**Step 8.** String the following beads: 3 carnelian, one 5mm silver, 1 aventurine, 1 garnet, 1 aventurine, one 5mm silver, 3 carnelian.

**Step 9.** String the following beads: 3 silver chips, one 6°, one 6mm silver, one 6°, 3 silver chips. Repeat Step 8 once.

**Step 10.** String the following beads: 3 silver chips, one 6°, 1 eye charm, one 6°, 3 silver chips.

**Step 11.** String the following beads: 1 carnelian, 1 garnet, 1 spiral charm, 1 garnet, 1 carnelian.

**Step 12.** Alternate Steps 10–11 twice as shown, then repeat Step 10.

**Step 13.** String the following beads: 1 carnelian, 1 aventurine, 1 garnet, the pendant, 1 garnet, 1 aventurine, 1 carnelian.

**Step 14.** Repeat Steps 8–13 in the reverse order so the second strand is symmetrical.

**Step 15.** Use a crimp tube to attach the wire end to the jump ring. Use wire cutters to cut off any extra wire. Attach a jump ring to each side of the clasp.

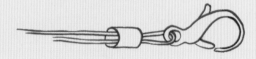

## USING CRIMPS TO ATTACH A CLASP

### Using a crimp tube

**1. Pass the wire end** through a crimp tube and half of the clasp, then pass it back through the crimp tube.

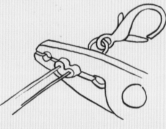

**2. Use a crimping tool to crimp** the tube. The crimping tool has an inner and an outer jaw. Use the inner jaw first to crease the tube.

**3. Next, use the outer jaw to fold** the tube in half. Doing so gives the crimp tube a secure and more professional finish than flattening it with chain-nose pliers.

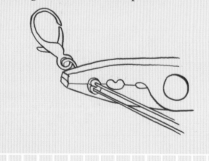

### Using a crimp end

**1. Place a crimp end** on the end of the wire.

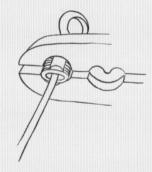

**2. Use chain-nose pliers or a crimping tool** to squeeze the sides together and flatten the inner coil.

**3. Use a jump ring or split ring** to attach the clasp.

The layered look is in—and it's so simple to create!

■ VARIATION

Designer-look jewelry doesn't have to break the bank. This aqua, blue, and green piece uses inexpensive, mass-produced metal castings and Czech glass beads. If you see a project you like but can't afford to make, use beads with a similar look but a smaller price tag.

## TIME TO BEAD
# WATCH

Beaded watches are the perfect combination
of fun and function. Combine bumpy
lampworked beads with textured
silver spacers for a bold, splashy
timepiece or mix gemstones
and glass beads for a subtle,
elegant version. Why not
make a watch for every day
of the week?

## ■ MATERIALS

- Silver 20mm rectangular watch face with loops
- 6 assorted10–12mm lampworked glass beads
- 6 aqua 4mm round glass beads
- 8 silver 8mm spacer beads
- Silver toggle clasp
- 2 silver crimp tubes
- 14" of beading wire

## ■ TOOLS

- Wire cutters
- Crimping tool

## ■ FINISHED SIZE

7½" (19 cm)

**Step 1.** Use wire cutters to cut the length of beading wire in half.

**Step 2.** Pass one length of beading wire through a loop on the watch face.

**Step 3.** Pass each end of the wire through 1 aqua bead.

**Step 4.** Hold the wire ends together and pass them through 1 silver bead and 1 lampworked bead; repeat two more times.

**Step 5.** Pass the wire ends through 1 silver bead, 1 aqua bead, 1 crimp tube, and half of the clasp.

**Step 6.** Pass the wire ends back through the crimp tube and the aqua bead.

**Step 7.** Use a crimping tool to crimp the crimp tube. Use wire cutters to cut off any extra wire. (see page 28)

**Step 8.** Repeat Steps 2–7 to complete the other side of the watch.

■ **VARIATION**
Garnet chips and rose-colored glass beads are a pretty color combination that can be worn with casual or dressy outfits. Try black/silver or gold/copper for a versatile watch for everyday wear.

## HELPFUL HINTS FOR MAKING WATCHES

■ **Watchbands must be extremely flexible.** Leave a little bit of space near the crimp so the band bends easily.

■ **Large beads affect the flexibility.** Use small spacers between big beads so the band will bend freely.

■ **Test the watchband before crimping** to make sure it's flexible enough.

■ **When you use large beads,** allow a little extra length to ensure the proper fit. (For example, the lampworked watch is 7½" [19 cm] long and fits a 7" [18 cm] wrist.)

■ **To make an interchangeable watchband,** attach a jump ring to each loop on the watch face. Attach one end of the watchband to one of the jump rings and the other end to a small clasp. Fasten the clasp to the other jump ring.

■ **Stretchy watches are also fun.** Use heavy stretchy jewelry cord to string the beads. Thread the ends back through all the beads so the cord is doubled, then tie it in a knot.

# FIT-FOR-A-QUEEN
# BRACELET

A beautiful focal bead deserves the royal treatment. Multiple seed-bead strands provide luster, and Bali silver spacers add a touch of class. Wear this bracelet and become queen for a day!

## ■ MATERIALS

- Red/purple/gold 25mm borosilicate glass bead
- 2 gold 12mm borosilicate glass beads
- 4 Bali silver 12mm disk beads
- 11° seed beads: 68 purple, 136 brown, 68 red
- 2 matte red 6° seed beads

- 2 silver 12mm cones
- Silver lobster clasp
- 5mm silver jump ring
- 2 silver crimp tubes
- 64" (162.5 cm) of beading wire
- Adhesive tape

## ■ TOOLS

- Wire cutters
- Chain-nose pliers

## ■ FINISHED SIZE

- 7" (18 cm)

**Step 1.** Use wire cutters to cut the beading wire into four equal lengths.

**Step 2.** Hold the wires together as one and pass them through 1 crimp tube, 1 cone, 1 red 6°, and the clasp.

**Step 3.** Pass the wire end back through the red 6° bead, cone, and crimp tube.

**Step 4.** Use chain-nose pliers to reach into the cone and gently flatten the crimp tube.

**Step 5.** String 34 beads of one color onto a wire. Use the end of the beading wire, not your fingers, to pick up the beads and place them on the wire.

**Step 6.** Attach a small piece of adhesive tape to prevent the beads from sliding off the end.

**Step 7.** Repeat Step 5 to make one purple strand, one red strand, and two brown strands.

**Step 8.** Remove the adhesive tape from the strands and string the following beads: 1 silver, 1 gold, 1 silver, large focal bead, 1 silver, 1 gold, 1 silver.

**Step 9.** String 34 beads of one color onto each wire, attaching a small piece of tape to keep beads from sliding off the ends.

**Step 10.** Remove the adhesive tape from the strands and string 1 crimp tube, 1 cone, 1 red 6°, and a jump ring onto the wire.

**Step 11.** Pass the wire end back through the red 6° bead, cone, and crimp tube.

**Step 12.** Adjust the wires so the crimp tube fits snugly inside the cone.

**Step 13.** Use chain-nose pliers to reach into the cone and gently flatten the crimp tube.

**Step 14.** Use wire cutters to cut off any extra wire.

*Show off a beautiful handmade bead.*

## ALL ABOUT ART GLASS

Mass-manufactured art glass beads are widely available, but part of the fun of beading is finding special handmade treasures at local bead shops and shows. Many artisans have made a name for themselves in the beading world by consistently producing high-quality, innovative glass beads. Here are some of the materials and techniques that make art glass beads special:

■ **Borosilicate:** Borosilicate is a very strong type of glass that withstands high heat. A common brand name for borosilicate is Pyrex. Borosilicate beads are very durable and tend to come in a subtler color palette than other lampworked beads.

■ **Dichroic:** The technology to make dichroic glass was originally used in aerospace, photography, and other industries, but it is now commonly used to make dynamic art and jewelry pieces. It's a true combination of art and science. The glass is sold in preformed sheets that are covered in a thin film of metal oxide. The vibrant colors are a result of the metal oxide coating: each metal yields a specific color. The oxides absorb and reflect light at different rates to give the glass an iridescent rainbowlike effect. A glass artist layers dichroic glass with ordinary glass to create a sparkly effect. Each artist combines the layers in different ways to make one-of-a-kind beads.

■ **Furnace:** Also called cane-glass beads, furnace beads are made by wrapping molten glass around a rod, then drawing the glass out into a tube that is sliced into sections to create individual beads. Many furnace beads have a series of stripes around the hole because the colors are stretched as the tube is formed.

■ **Lampworked:** Also called flameworked, lampworked beads are produced by heating glass with a torch, wrapping the melted glass around a rod, and annealing the finished beads in a kiln. Lampworked beads can be as different as the artist who creates them. Some are bright and bumpy while others have dimensional floral patterns or smooth swirls of colors. Sometimes a powdery white residue (release agent) is left inside the beads. Use a bead reamer to clean the holes; rinse the beads before you string them.

# NECKLACE AND BRACELET

This gorgeous combination is one part necklace and one part bracelet. Just attach the toggle clasps together to wear both pieces as a necklace. It's two for one!

*Wear them separately or attach them together to make a long necklace.*

35

## ■ MATERIALS

### NECKLACE

16" (40.5 cm) strand of 4mm
   rose quartz round beads

16" (40.5 cm) strand of
   6mm garnet chips

16" (40.5 cm) strand of
   6mm light green
   freshwater pearls

1 silver "Spirit" ring

1 Bali silver toggle clasp

6 silver crimp tubes

2 silver 6mm jump rings

4¹/₂" (11.5 cm) of silver small
   cable chain

54" (137 cm) of beading wire

### BRACELET

8 rose quartz 6mm
   round beads

10 garnet 6mm
   faceted buttons

2 light green pearl 8mm round
   crystal beads

1 Bali silver 14mm round bead

4 Bali silver 5mm disks

1 Bali silver toggle clasp

2 silver crimp tubes

9" (23 cm) of beading wire

## ■ TOOLS

Chain-nose pliers

Wire cutters

Crimping tool

## ■ FINISHED SIZE

Necklace: 19" (48.5 cm)

Bracelet: 7" (18 cm)

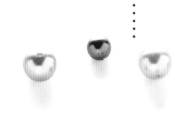

## ■ NECKLACE

**Step 1.** Use wire cutters to cut the beading wire in three equal lengths.

**Step 2.** Use wire cutters to cut the chain in six equal lengths.

**Step 3.** Use a crimp tube to attach a length of beading wire to a length of chain. Use a crimping tool to crimp the tube. (see page 28)

**Step 4.** Pass the wire end through all the beads of one type.

**Step 5.** Use a crimp tube to attach the wire end to a length of chain as in Step 3.

**Step 6.** Use chain-nose pliers to open a jump ring and attach it to the last chain link on each end of the beaded strand.

**Step 7.** Attach half of the clasp to the jump ring on each end of the beaded strand.

**Step 8.** Repeat Steps 3–7 to make two more beaded strands.

**Step 9.** Pass the toggle bar through the "Spirit" ring to string the ring onto the necklace.

## ■ BRACELET

**Step 1.** Use a crimp tube to attach half of the clasp to the end of the beading wire.

**Step 2.** String the following beads: 4 rose quartz, 1 silver disk, 1 pearl, 1 silver disk, 5 garnet.

**Step 3.** String the 14mm Bali silver bead.

**Step 4.** Repeat Steps 1–2 in the reverse order so the bracelet is symmetrical.

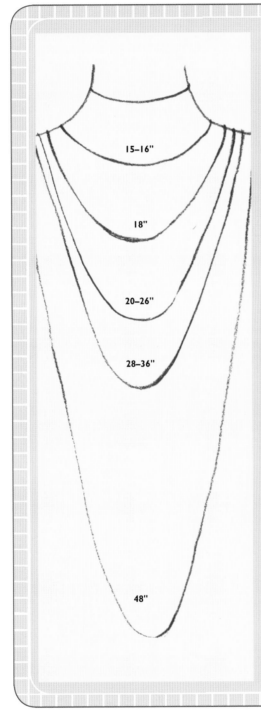

## STANDARD JEWELRY LENGTHS
Choker: 15–16" (38–40.5 cm)
Princess necklace: 18" (45.5 cm)
Matinee necklace: 20–26" (51–61 cm)
Opera necklace: 28–36" (61–91.5 cm)
Lariat: 36–48"
Bracelet: 7–8" (18–20.5 cm)

## Approximate Number of Beads in a 16" Strand:

| | | | |
|---|---|---|---|
| 4mm | 101 | 10mm | 40 |
| 6mm | 67 | 12mm | 33 |
| 8mm | 50 | | |

## Adjusting the Length:

■ **Sometimes you have the perfect necklace** or bracelet, but it stays stashed in a drawer because it just isn't the right length. Well, bring it out into the light! There are lots of ways to adjust the length.

■ **To lengthen a design,** add an extension chain. Decide how much length you want to add, then cut a piece of chain that length. Fasten the last chain link to the end opposite the clasp. Then fasten the clasp anywhere along the chain. This is also an easy way to make any design adjustable.

■ **To shorten a design,** it is necessary to cut off the clasp. Then you can just remove some of the beads and reattach the clasp at the desired length. Before you cut the piece, make sure that there will be at least 2" of extra stringing material to reattach the clasp, otherwise you will need to restring the design.

■ **To convert a bracelet into a necklace,** add pieces of suede cord or chain to the ends of the bracelet. Attach a clasp to the other end of the suede cord or chain.

■ **If you need to restring your design,** take a picture or scan of the piece before you disassemble it. That way you'll be sure to get the pattern just right when you restring it.

# LUSCIOUS
# LARIAT

A lariat is a dramatic piece that can be worn as a long necklace, a choker, or even a belt. It can go dressy or casual, and it adds instant flair to any outfit.

**Step 1.** String 1 silver disk, 1 crystal bead, and 1 silver disk onto a head pin.

**Step 2.** Make a wrapped loop above the top bead, wrapping the wire seven to eight times around the stem. (see page 47)

**Step 3.** Repeat Steps 1–2 to make another beaded head pin.

**Step 4.** Pass the wire end through a crimp bead and a beaded head-pin loop.

**Step 5.** Pass the wire end back through the crimp bead to form a small loop. Crimp it. (see page 28)

**Step 6.** String the following beads onto the wire: 1 labradorite rondelle, 3 pearls, 1 bead cap, 1 red aventurine.

**Step 7.** String 1 Bali tube, then repeat Step 5 in the reverse order.

*Lariats are so versatile and stylish . . .*

## ■ MATERIALS

11 tanzanite 8mm faceted
    round crystal beads
40 labradorite 5mm faceted
    rondelle beads
40 lavender 4mm
    freshwater pearls
20 red aventurine 6mm
    round beads
5 Bali silver 12mm
    round beads

5 Bali silver 10mm tube beads
10 Bali silver 5mm
    coiled beads
10 Bali silver 5mm bead caps
22 Bali silver 5mm disk beads
2 sterling silver 2" (5 cm)
    head pins
40 silver crimp beads
46" (117 cm) length of .018"
    silver beading wire

## ■ TOOLS

Round-nose pliers
Chain-nose pliers
Wire cutters
Crimping tool

## ■ FINISHED SIZE

One size fits all

**Step 8.** String a crimp bead onto the wire. Place it snugly against the last labradorite bead. Crimp it.

**Step 9.** Leave 1" (2.5 cm), then attach another crimp bead. String 1 silver disk, 1 crystal bead, 1 silver disk, and 1 crimp bead. Crimp it.

**Step 10.** Leave 1" (2.5 cm), then attach another crimp bead. String the following beads: 1 pearl, 3 labradorite rondelles, 1 silver coil, 1 red aventurine.

**Step 11.** String 1 Bali round, then repeat Step 10 in the reverse order.

**Step 12.** String a crimp bead onto the wire. Place it snugly against the last pearl. Crimp it.

**Step 13.** Repeat Step 9.

**Step 14.** Repeat Steps 6–13 four times and then repeat Steps 6–8 one more time.

**Step 15.** Pass the wire end through a crimp bead and a beaded head-pin loop.

**Step 16.** Pass the wire end back through the crimp bead to form a small loop. Crimp it.

■ **VARIATION**

Create an illusion-style necklace by using the same technique to crimp square freshwater pearl beads in place on the beading wire. To ensure even spacing, cut a length of rubber tubing or a drinking straw to the right length. Slip it onto the wire between beaded sections to determine where to attach the next crimp bead, then remove it and string the beads.

*The beads just seem to float on your neck.*

## COMMON BEADING PATTERNS

■ **Asymmetrical Patterns:** Slightly difficult to achieve successfully, asymmetrical patterns have an eclectic, artsy look. Pay special attention to the actual weight of the beads so the design is balanced on both sides even though it isn't visually symmetrical; otherwise the piece may shift while worn.

■ **Random Patterns:** Our eyes like to make order out of chaos, so a collection of randomly strung beads actually creates a patterned effect. For best results, manipulate the randomness a little to make sure that identical beads are not next to each other.

■ **Repeating Patterns:** The simplest patterns are just two beads repeating one after the other. Make the pattern more complex by adding more beads and interesting metal spacers.

■ **Symmetrical Patterns:** Symmetry gives a beaded design a soothing, sometimes classic feel. Place a focal bead or pendant in the center of a jewelry design, then string a symmetrical bead pattern on each side.

# IN VOGUE
# PURSE

Add some pizzazz to a store-bought purse with dazzling beaded strands and purse charms. It's an easy, fashionable way to express your own style.

## ■ MATERIALS

### BEADED STRANDS

33 tanzanite 4mm faceted
    round crystal beads
6 tanzanite 8mm crystal cubes
5 brown 10mm wooden tubes
7 brown 10mm wooden
    round beads
5 tiger's eye 8mm
    round beads
30 tiger's eye 4mm
    round beads
10 gray 4mm
    freshwater pearls
10 Bali silver 5mm
    spacer beads
14 Bali silver 6mm
    spacer beads
2 silver 20mm split rings
4 silver crimp tubes
28" (71. cm) of beading wire

### PURSE CHARM

Heliotrope 20mm crystal cross
Bali silver 15mm round bead
Tiger's eye 30mm disk
Aquamarine 4mm faceted
    bicone crystal bead
3" (7.5 cm) length of
    silver chain
Silver 2" (5 cm) plain head pin
Silver 2" (5 cm) decorative
    head pin
3 silver 6mm jump rings
Silver 8mm jump ring
Large silver lobster clasp

## ■ TOOLS

Round-nose pliers
Chain-nose pliers
Wire cutters
Crimping tool

## ■ FINISHED SIZE

Beaded strands: 11½" (29 cm)
    and 12½" (31.5 cm)
Purse charms: 4¼" (11 cm)

## ■ BEADED STRANDS

**Step 1.** Cut the beading wire into one 13½"
(34.5 cm) and one 15½" (39.5 cm) length.
**Step 2.** Use a crimp tube to attach the 13½"
(34.5 cm) length to a 20mm split ring. (see page 28)
**Step 3.** String the following beads: 3 round crystals, 1
wooden tube, 3 round crystals, one 5mm spacer,
1 pearl, one 6mm tiger's eye, 1 pearl, one 5mm spacer;
repeat four more times.
**Step 4.** Pass the wire end through 3 round crystals.
**Step 5.** Use a crimp tube to attach the wire end to a
20mm split ring.
**Step 6.** Use a crimp tube to attach the 15½" length below
the first strand on a 20mm split ring and string three
4mm tiger's eye beads onto the second strand.
**Step 7.** String the following beads: one 6mm spacer, one
10mm wooden, one 6mm spacer, two 4mm tiger's eye,
1 crystal cube, two 4mm tiger's eye; repeat five
more times.
**Step 8.** String the following beads: one 6mm spacer, one
10mm wooden, one 6mm spacer, three 4mm tiger's eye.
**Step 9.** Use a crimp tube to attach the wire end below the
first strand on the second 20mm split ring.
**Step 10.** To attach the beaded strands to a purse, connect
the split rings to the base of the straps.

## ■ PURSE CHARMS

**Step 1.** Cut the following chain lengths: ½", 1½",
1" (1.3, 3.8, 2.5 cm)
**Step 2.** Use chain-nose pliers to open an 8mm
jump ring and connect it to the crystal cross;
attach the jump ring to the last link on the
½" (1.3 cm) chain.
**Step 3.** String the tiger's eye disk onto a
decorative head pin. Make a wrapped loop to
attach it to the last link on the 1½" (3.8) chain.
(see page 47)
**Step 4.** String the aquamarine crystal and one
15mm silver bead onto a plain head pin. Make a
wrapped loop to attach it to the last link on the
1" (2.5 cm) chain.
**Step 5.** Connect a 6mm jump ring to the upper
link on each length of chain.
**Step 6.** Attach the jump rings to the lobster clasp
with the longest chain in the center.

# GETTING WIRED

# FROM THE MOST BASIC LOOPS

to more complicated bead links, wireworking is a fundamental part of making jewelry and beaded accessories. ■ Wireworking can be intimidating for beginners, but it gets easier with practice. I promise! Perfect your technique with inexpensive base metal before moving on to more expensive metals like sterling silver.

## QUICK AND EASY
# EARRINGS

Depending on your mood, earrings can complement a necklace or stand on their own. Use different beads from those specified to create an even more casual or glamorous pair. It just takes a couple of simple techniques and less than half an hour to make pretty earrings that you'll wear every day.

10-minute

■ **10-MINUTE EARRINGS**
**Step 1.** Place 1 bead cap over the hole on 1 yellow bead so it fits like a hat.
**Step 2.** String the yellow bead and bead cap onto a head pin.
**Step 3.** Make a wrapped loop to attach the head pin to an ear wire. (see next page)
**Step 4.** Repeat Steps 1–3 to make a matching earring.

■ **15-MINUTE EARRINGS**
**Step 1.** Attach an eye pin loop to an ear wire.
**Step 2.** String the following beads onto the wire: 1 red aventurine, 1 silver disk, 1 pearl.
**Step 3.** Use the middle of the round-nose pliers to make a medium-size loop on the end of the eye pin. (see next page)
**Step 4.** String a leaf bead onto the lower loop.
**Step 5.** Repeat Steps 1–4 to make a matching earring.

*Whip up these earrings in an evening.*

15-minute

30-minute

## ■ MATERIALS

### 10-MINUTE EARRINGS

2 yellow 8mm firepolished
    round glass beads
2 silver 8mm bead caps
2 silver 2" (5 cm) head pins
2 silver decorative ear wires

### 15-MINUTE EARRINGS

2 red aventurine
    4mm round beads
2 light green pearl
    8mm round crystal beads
2 silver 6mm disks
2 silver 10mm leaf beads
2 silver 2" (5 cm) eye pins
2 silver decorative ear wires

### 30-MINUTE EARRINGS

2 topaz 6mm firepolished
    round glass beads
4 red aventurine
    4mm round beads
4 carnelian
    4mm round beads
2 green aventurine
    6mm round beads
2 silver figure-eight earring
    components
2 silver 5mm jump rings
10 silver 1" (2.5 cm)
    head pins
2 silver 1½" (3.8 cm)
    head pins
2 silver decorative ear wires

## ■ TOOLS

Round-nose pliers
Chain-nose pliers
Wire cutters

## ■ FINISHED SIZE

As desired.

## ■ 30-MINUTE EARRINGS

**Step 1.** Use chain-nose pliers to open a jump ring. Use it to connect a figure-eight earring component to an ear wire.

**Step 2.** String one 6mm topaz bead onto a 1½" (3.8 cm) head pin.

**Step 3.** Make a large basic loop above the topaz bead and attach it to the center of a figure-eight component. (see right)

**Step 4.** String 1 red aventurine bead onto a 1" (2.5 cm) head pin and attach it to the first and fifth loops on the figure-eight component.

**Step 5.** String 1 carnelian bead onto a 1" (2.5 cm) head pin and attach one to the second and fourth loops on the figure-eight component.

**Step 6.** String 1 green aventurine bead onto a 1" (2.5 cm) head pin and attach it to the third loop on the figure-eight component.

**Step 7.** Repeat Steps 1–6 to make a matching earring.

## MAKING WIRE LOOPS

### ■ Basic loop:

Basic and wrapped loops are often used to attach beaded dangles to earrings or a necklace. Basic loops are best for designs that will not bear a lot of weight, such as lightweight earrings. Wrapped loops are a more secure choice because they will not accidentally pull open; they're best for weightier pieces such as necklaces.

1. Make a right angle about ½" (1.3 cm) from the end of the wire.
2. Place the center of the round-nose pliers next to the angle, positioned on the short length of wire.
3. Wrap the short wire end over the top of the pliers to form a loop.
4. Cut off any extra wire.

### ■ Wrapped loop:

1. Make a right angle about 1" (2.5 cm) from the end of the wire.
2. Place the center of the round-nose pliers next to the angle, positioned on the short length of wire.
3. Wrap the short wire end over the top of the pliers to form a loop.
4. Wrap the wire end tightly around the base of the loop to create two or three coils.

## SPARKLY BEADED
# BARRETTES

These simple hair accessories are a snap to make. Use wire to attach metal sliders and crystal beads to a clip-style barrette. Your friends will probably be jealous of your sparkly headgear, so you'd better make extras!

■ **VARIATION**
Use inspirational word sliders to make a thoughtful version of the same barrette. Or make a super sparkly variation with crystal beads in mixed colors and sizes. Try the same technique with gemstone chips for an earthier look or with round glass beads for an inexpensive version.

## ■ MATERIALS

- 2 silver 14mm metal sliders with inset rose crystals
- 2 silver 16mm metal sliders with inset rose crystals
- 16 rose 4mm bicone crystal beads

- 12" (30.5 cm) length of 24-gauge silver wire
- 3" silver clip barrette with holes on the ends

## ■ TOOLS

- Chain-nose pliers
- Wire cutters

## ■ FINISHED SIZE

- 3" (7.5 cm)

**Step 1.** Center the wire inside a hole on the barrette.

**Step 2.** Wrap the wire two to three times around the outer edge of the barrette, ending with the wire ends on the front of the barrette.

**Step 3.** Pass each wire end through 1 crystal bead.

**Step 4.** Pass each wire end through a hole on a 14mm metal slider.

**Step 5.** Pass each wire end through 2 crystal beads and cross the wires between the 2 crystal beads.

**Step 6.** Pass the wire ends through a hole on a 16mm metal slider.

**Step 7.** Repeat Steps as follows: 5, 4, 5, 6, and 3.

**Step 8.** Place the wire ends through the hole on the end of the barrette.

**Step 9.** Wrap the wire two to three times around the outer edge of the barrette, ending with the wire ends on the back of the barrette.

**Step 10.** Twist the wire ends together and use chain-nose pliers to press them firmly into the back of the barrette. Cut off any extra wire.

*These sparkly barrettes are super simple to make.*

## ROCK 'N ROLL
# CUFF

A little bit of rock 'n roll and a whole lot of fabulous, this cuff is sure to turn some heads. You'll perfect your basic wire coiling and bead stringing skills, and you'll end up with this show-stopping cuff.

*Indulge your inner rock star with this funky cuff.*

## ■ MATERIALS

- Suede or leather cuff bracelet with snap, 1¼" wide
- 4 painted silk 25mm tube beads: teal, yellow, olive, purple
- 2 topaz 8mm faceted round crystal beads
- 2 indicolite 8mm bicone crystal beads
- 1 tanzanite 8mm faceted round crystal bead
- 1 light Colorado topaz 8mm cube crystal bead
- 3 light gray pearl 8mm crystal beads
- 8 black pearl 8mm round crystal beads
- 6 Bali silver 6mm rondelles
- 28 clear/silver 6° seed beads
- 28" (61 cm) length of 24-gauge sterling silver wire

## ■ TOOLS

- Round-nose pliers
- Chain-nose pliers
- Wire cutters

## ■ FINISHED SIZE

As desired

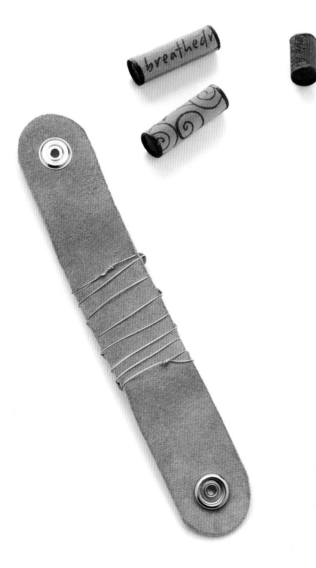

**Step 1.** Hold the end of the wire against the back of the cuff and wrap the wire once around the cuff.

**Step 2.** Use round-nose pliers to coil the end of the wire around the first full wrap. Use chain-nose pliers to press the end of the wire flat against the coil.

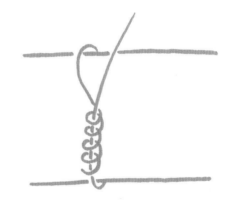

**Step 3.** String 1 dark gray pearl and 7 size 6° seed beads onto the wire.

**Step 4.** Slide a silk tube over the seed beads, then string another dark gray pearl onto the wire and wrap the wire around the cuff. The seed beads prevent the pearls from sliding inside the large holes of the silk tubes.

**Step 5.** String a collection of crystals, silver beads, and a light gray pearl onto the wire and wrap the wire around the cuff. (See image at left).

**Step 6.** Repeat Steps 4–5 two more times, then Repeat Step 4.

**Step 7.** Wrap the wire once around the cuff.

**Step 8.** Use round-nose pliers to coil the end of the wire around the last full wrap. Use chain-nose pliers to press the end of the wire flat against the coil.

# Y NOT?
# NECKLACE

This perennial necklace style has a delicate look that's elegant enough for evening but simple enough for daytime. Use elongated chain for a funkier spin or larger chain for an edgier look. Wear it with a V-neck or scoop-neck top—Y Not?

**Step 1.** Use wire cutters to cut the chain into these lengths: one 1" (2.5 cm), four 1½" (3.8 cm), two 2¼" (5.5 cm).

**Step 2.** String 1 crystal onto an eye pin. Make a basic loop and attach it to the clasp. Repeat this step and attach it to the other side of the clasp. (see page 47)

**Step 3.** Attach a 2¼" (5.5 cm) length of chain to each beaded eye pin from Step 2.

**Step 4.** String 1 crystal, 1 bead cap, 1 cube, 1 bead cap, and 1 crystal onto a 2" (5 cm) eye pin. Make a basic loop after the last bead. Repeat this step six times.

**Step 5.** Attach a beaded eye pin from Step 4 to the end of the 2¼" (5.5 cm) chains. String a 1½" (3.2 cm) length of chain onto the other side of the beaded eye pin.

**Step 6.** Connect a beaded eye pin to the end of the chains from Step 5. Attach a 1½" (3.8 cm) length of chain to the other end of the beaded eye pin.

**Step 7.** Attach a beaded eye pin to the end of the chain from Step 6. Use a 4mm jump ring to connect the two beaded eye pins in the center of the necklace. Attach a 1" (2.5 cm) length of chain to the jump ring.

**Step 8.** String the garnet and silver connector onto another jump ring and connect the jump ring to the other end of the 1" (2.5 cm) length of chain.

**Step 9.** String 1 bead cap, 1 cube, and 1 bead cap onto a 1" (2.5 cm) eye pin. Make a basic loop. Attach one end of the beaded eye pin to the garnet and silver pendant and one end to the hill tribe pendant.

**Step 10.** String 1 crystal onto a head pin. Make a basic loop to attach it to the hill tribe pendant.

*Simple, elegant, and eye-catching . . .*

## ■ MATERIALS

- 7 burgundy 6mm Czech glass cube beads
- 15 light rose 4mm faceted round crystal beads
- 14 Bali silver 6mm bead caps
- Silver 20mm connector with inset garnet cabochon
- Hill tribe silver 20mm pendant

- 7 silver 2" (5 cm) eye pins
- 2 silver 1" (2.5 cm) eye pins
- 1 silver ½" (1.3 cm) head pin
- 2 silver 4mm jump rings
- Silver lobster clasp
- 11½" of silver small cable chain

## ■ TOOLS

- Round-nose pliers
- Chain-nose pliers
- Wire cutters

## ■ FINISHED SIZE

- 21" (53.5 cm)

### HILL TRIBE SILVER

■ **Although it is sometimes called "Thai silver,"** hill tribe silver is made by a variety of tribes who live in the region where Thailand, Burma, and Laos come together. The six major tribes are the Karen (Kariang, Yang), the Hmong (Meo), the Yao (Mien), the Akha (Ekaw), the Lisu (Lisaw), and the Lahu (Mussur).

■ **All the tribes work at farming,** but they're also renowned silversmiths. The silversmith skill is traditionally passed from generation to generation. As modern society encroaches, it has become more and more important for hill tribe people to be able to make money from their craft. The popularity of hill tribe silver beads means that the tribes have been able to preserve their artisan culture because people can afford to stay in the villages rather than go to the cities to find work.

■ **Hill tribe silver beads are made by hand.** Similar design elements may be used, but you'll notice that no two pieces are exactly alike. Hill tribe motifs are inspired by nature and include dragonflies, flowers, and seashells. Hill tribe silver beads and components often have a very organic look and combine beautifully with gemstones or handmade glass beads.

■ **Sterling Silver has a minimum fine silver content of 92.5 percent,** but most hill tribe silver has a higher fine silver content, closer to 99 percent. Store this silver in an airtight container and use a polishing cloth to restore its luster.

## CHA-CHA
# BRACELET

This funky and fabulous design will make you want
to dance around, just so you can hear that "cha-cha"
sound! A cha-cha or expansion bracelet looks like a
watchband, but it has little loops on each section for
attaching beaded head pins. Create all the beaded head
pins first (while watching TV, perhaps) and then attach
them to the bracelet.

Make your own music with this spunky bracelet.

■ **MATERIALS**

14 of each color 6–8mm round fire-polished beads: light blue, green, lavender

Czech glass beads in assorted shapes: light blue, green, lavender

Silver 3-row expansion bracelet

42 silver 1" (2.5 cm) head pins

84 silver 1½" (3.8 cm) head pins

■ **TOOLS**

Round-nose pliers
Chain-nose pliers
Wire cutters

■ **FINISHED SIZE**

One size fits all

■ **VARIATION**

A one-row expansion bracelet is quick to assemble and still makes that satisfying cha-cha sound. Save time by purchasing multicolored glass or gemstone bead mixes. This variation features mixed barrel and rondelle semiprecious moonkite (moukaite) beads. The variegated colors of moonkite beads create an easy, natural mix. Other inherently multicolored gemstones like fluorite, Indian jasper, or tourmaline would work well, too.

**Step 1.** String each fire-polished bead onto a 1" (2.5 cm) head pin. Make a basic loop above the bead. (see page 47)

**Step 2.** String ½" (1.3 cm) of same-color, assorted shape Czech glass beads onto each 1½" (3.8 cm) head pin. Make a basic loop above the beads.

**Step 3.** Prepare all the loops for attaching to the bracelet by using chain-nose pliers to open them. (Remember to twist the loops open instead of pulling the ends directly apart.)

**Step 4.** Attach 1 fire-polished bead to each section of the bracelet, alternating colors and position on the sections.

**Step 5.** Attach the assorted Czech glass beads at even spaces across the bracelet. Part of the appeal of the finished bracelet is its jumbled-up, random mix of colors and shapes, so don't stress too much about the placement of the beads.

**Step 6.** Slide the finished bracelet onto your wrist and shake it like mad!

## ■ MATERIALS

- 24 indicolite 4mm bicone crystal beads
- 2 Bali silver 8mm round beads
- 2 silver 6mm oval jump rings
- 2 silver 1½" (3.8 cm) head pins
- 2 silver 2" (5 cm) eye pins
- 16" of silver small cable chain
- 2 silver ear wires

## ■ TOOLS

- Round-nose pliers
- Chain-nose pliers
- Wire cutters

## ■ FINISHED SIZE

- 3" (7.5 cm)

## GLAMOUR GIRL
# CHANDELIERS

This hot fashion accessory isn't going away anytime soon. Store-bought components are widely available, or you can make your own from scratch, as I do. Your handcrafted chandeliers will add instant drama to any outfit!

**Step 1.** Use chain-nose pliers to open a jump ring and connect it to the lower loop on an ear wire.

**Step 2.** String 5 crystals, the jump ring/ear wire, and 5 more crystals onto an eye pin.

**Step 3.** Make a basic loop on the end of the eye pin. (see page 47)

**Step 4.** Cut three lengths of chain: 1, 3, 4" (2.5, 7.5, 10 cm).

**Step 5.** String the 3" (7.5 cm) and 4" (10 cm) lengths of chain onto the eye pin loops with the 3" (7.5 cm) chain on the inside.

**Step 6.** String 1 crystal, 1 Bali bead, and 1 crystal onto a head pin.

**Step 7.** Make a wrapped loop above the top bead to attach it to the last link on the 1" (2.5 cm) length of chain.

**Step 8.** Connect the top link on the 1" (2.5 cm) length of chain to the jump ring so it dangles in the center of the earring.

## ■ VARIATION

Linear earrings are a longer, leaner take on the chandelier. Combine gemstones or crystals with long chains to make shoulder-grazing stunners. This threader version uses crystal frames and wire-wrapped jump rings.

## ■ MATERIALS

- 30 red 4mm–8mm fire-polished glass beads
- 28" (71 cm) length of 26-gauge silver wire
- 29" (73.5 cm) length of 16-gauge silver wire
- 2½" (6.5 cm) clear glass candleholder

## ■ TOOLS

- Round-nose pliers
- Chain-nose pliers
- Wire cutters

## ■ FINISHED SIZE

- 2½" (6.5 cm) tall

## CLEVER CANDLE
# WRAP

Whether you buy glass beads especially for this purpose or use beads left over from another project, this candleholder rocks! Make one for every room in your house.

**Step 1.** Use round-nose pliers to make a loop on one end of the 16-gauge wire.

**Step 2.** Hold the loop between your thumb and forefinger and turn your wrist to make a three-turn spiral.

**Step 3.** Use round-nose pliers to make a loop on the other end of the wire.

**Step 4.** Wrap one end of the 26-gauge wire around the base of the spiral. Use chain-nose pliers to press the wire end firmly against the 16-gauge wire.

**Step 5.** Wrap the 26-gauge wire three to four times around the 16-gauge wire and string a bead.

**Step 6.** Wrap the 26-gauge wire three to four more times.

**Step 7.** String 1 bead and wrap the 26-gauge wire 3–4 more times, leaving a ¾–1" space between the beads. Continue this step until all the beads have been used, and the whole length of the 16-gauge wire is embellished.

**Step 8.** Hold the spiral against the candleholder and wrap the 16-gauge wire around the candleholder to make a loose coil. (To prevent overheating, make sure the wire doesn't touch the glass.)

*Candle wraps make great gifts.*

## MOD MILLEFIORI
# NECKLACE

Traditionally used to make rosaries, this simple technique also makes great fashion jewelry. Plus, the necklace is convertible. To wear it as a Y-style necklace, fasten the hook at the front of the neck with the end dangling down. To wear it as simple single-strand necklace, fasten it in the back.

*Perfect your wire-wrapping skills one link at a time.*

**Step 1.** Cut 36 silver 2½" (5 cm) lengths of wire.

**Step 2.** Make a wrapped loop on the end of a 2½" (5 cm) length of wire. (see page 47)

**Step 3.** Pass the wire end through 1 millefiori bead and make a wrapped loop on the other end.

**Step 4.** Repeat Steps 2–3 for all the millefiori beads.

**Step 5.** Begin a wrapped loop on the end of a 2½" (5 cm) length of wire. Before wrapping the base of the loop, connect the loop to a millefiori bead link.

**Step 6.** Repeat Step 5 to connect alternating millefiori and crystal beads.

**Step 7.** String each citrine bead onto a head pin and make wrapped loops to attach them to the end of the necklace.

**Step 8.** Use chain-nose pliers to open the hook loop and attach it to the other end of the necklace.

## ■ MATERIALS

- 13 red/yellow/aqua 10mm millefiori disk beads
- 13 Pacific opal 6mm faceted round crystal beads
- 2 citrine 8mm faceted buttons
- 90" length of 22-gauge sterling silver wire
- 2 sterling silver 1½" (3.8 cm) decorative head pins
- Sterling silver S-hook

## ■ TOOLS

- Round-nose pliers
- Chain-nose pliers
- Wire cutters

## ■ FINISHED SIZE

17½" (44.5 cm) adjustable

---

## MAKING BEAD LINKS

### ■ Plain bead links:

1. Cut a length of wire that's 2" (5 cm) longer than the bead.
2. Make a wrapped loop on one end. (see page 47)

3. String a bead.

4. Make another wrapped loop.

5. Use wire cutters to cut off any extra wire.

### ■ Decorative bead links:

1. Cut a length of wire that's 3–4" longer than the bead.
2. Make a wrapped loop on one end. (see page 47)

3. String a bead.

4. Make another wrapped loop, then wrap the remaining wire in a spiral or crisscross pattern around the bead.

5. Wrap the wire end tightly around the base of the first wrapped loop.

6. Use wire cutters to cut off any extra wire.

### ■ Connecting bead links:

1. Make a bead link.

2. Make a second bead link but do not wrap the second loop.

3. Connect the unwrapped loop to a loop on the first bead link.

4. Wrap the loop.

5. Use wire cutters to cut off any extra wire.

**Tip:** For faster assembly, wire-wrap all the beads of one style (the millefiori beads, for example). Then use the other beads (crystals) to link the first batch of beads (millefiori) together.

# KNOTTY BUT NICE

## KNOTS ARE TRADITIONALLY

used to separate pearls or gemstones, but beaders today are incorporating knotting into lots of different types of jewelry. ■ You can, too! ■ These projects put a hip twist on a centuries-old technique.

## KNOTTING BETWEEN BEADS

Pearls and other gemstones are traditionally knotted between the beads to keep the beads from rubbing against each other and to prevent loss if a strand should break. Contemporary jewelry designers are using the natural, comfortable look of knotted silk with a variety of beads to create unusual knotted designs. This practice is a perfect example of using a conventional technique in an unconventional way.

### ■ Getting started:

1. Choose 6 beads with holes that are large enough for the silk to pass through twice, or use a bead reamer to enlarge them.
2. Cut two ¼–¾" lengths of French wire.
3. Tie a knot 1" (2.5 cm) from the end of the silk and pass the needle through three beads.
4. Pass the needle and half of the clasp through a length of French wire.

5. Adjust the beads so there is about 2" (5 cm) of silk between the first bead and the knot at the end of the silk.

### ■ Making knots:

Knots are traditionally made by using a beading awl to work the knot into the proper position snugly against the bead. If you don't have an awl, you can use a stiff beading needle instead.
1. Follow the Getting started Steps 1–5 above.
2. Pass the needle back through the last bead and form a loose overhand knot.
3. Put the end of the awl inside the knot and pull the thread to tighten the knot, keeping the awl tightly against the bead.

4. Tighten the knot and remove the awl.
5. String 2 more beads and tie a knot between them and after the last one.
6. Place a drop of jeweler's glue on the last knot. Let it dry, then cut off the short thread end.
7. String and knot the remaining beads except for the last three, then follow Finishing the strand Steps 1–5.

### ■ Finishing the strand:

1. Once all the beads are knotted except for the last 3, pass the needle through those last 3 beads, the French wire, and half of the clasp.
2. Pass the needle back through the last bead.
3. Adjust the beads so there is just enough room between them to allow adequate space for each knot.
4. Make a knot between the last few beads.
5. Place a drop of jeweler's cement on the final knot. Let it dry, then cut off any extra thread.

TIP
### Knotting with a knotting tool:

A knotting tool makes it easy to get tight, consistent knots. Using the tool takes a little practice, but it is well worth it if you're planning to do a lot of knotting. It's much quicker than knotting by hand. Knotting tools come with extensive instructions.

# WORLD BEAT
# CHOKER

Use beads from around the world to make this dramatic tasseled choker. A handmade lampworked bead, Mexican dichroic beads, Japanese cube beads, Austrian crystals, and Thai silver beads all add up to an eclectic international look.

## ■ MATERIALS

- Cream/magenta/lavender 40mm borosilicate lampworked bead
- 2 magenta 10mm large-hole dichroic glass beads
- 2 burgundy 4mm faceted round crystal beads
- 4 burgundy 6mm faceted round crystal beads
- 2 tanzanite 4mm faceted round crystal beads
- 2 amethyst 4mm faceted round crystal beads
- 6 Hill tribe silver 6mm faceted cube beads
- 3 Hill tribe silver 8mm round beads
- 6 Hill tribe silver 6mm disks
- 11 gold-red 4mm cube beads
- 2 silver 5mm round memory-wire end caps
- 2 black 7½" (19 cm) lengths of 2.5mm diameter rubber tubing
- 1½" continuous loops of necklace-size memory wire
- 5" (12.5 cm) length of 22-gauge sterling silver wire
- 3 black 12" (30.5 cm) lengths of 1.5mm black leather cord
- 2 black 12" (30.5 cm) lengths of #4 silk cord
- Epoxy
- Jeweler's cement

## ■ TOOLS

- Round-nose pliers
- Chain-nose pliers
- Wire cutters
- Large-eye beading needle

## ■ FINISHED SIZE

One size fits all

**Step 1.** Hold the leather and silk cords together and tie them in an overhand knot.

**Step 2.** Make a loop on one end of the silver wire.

**Step 3.** Thread the loop through the knot, then wrap the loop.

**Step 4.** Place a drop of jeweler's cement on the knot.

**Step 5.** Pass the wire end through 1 large-hole dichroic glass bead to cover the knot.

**Step 6.** Pass the wire end through 1 borosilicate bead, 1 dichroic bead, and one 8mm silver bead.

**Step 7.** Make a wrapped loop above the last bead.

**Step 8.** String the wire loop onto the center of the memory wire.

**Step 9.** String beads as follows on each side of the necklace: two 6mm burgundy, one 6mm silver faceted cube, 2 gold-red cubes, one 6mm silver disk, 1 amethyst bicone, 1 silver disk, 2 gold-red cubes.

**Step 10.** Pass each memory wire end through a length of rubber tubing.

**Step 11.** Use epoxy to glue 1 silver disk and a memory-wire end cap onto each end of the wire.

**Step 12.** String the remaining beads randomly onto the cord ends as shown. Tie overhand knots to hold them in place.

**Step 13.** Cut the cord ends at slightly uneven levels to add interest to the tassel.

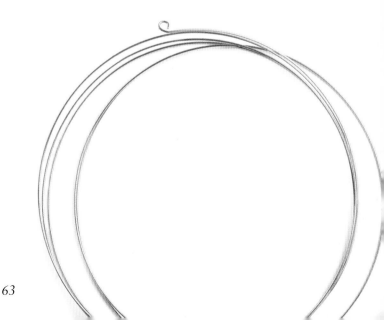

# CENTER STAGE OPERA
# NECKLACE

Make a dramatic entrance with this long, alluring necklace. Opera necklaces traditionally end at or just below the waistline, but they may wrap two or three times around the neck for a short and sweet look.

Combine the soft texture of suede with the metallic edge of chain.

## ■ MATERIALS

6 purple/aqua/green 6mm
  round lampworked glass
  beads
6 amethyst 4mm bicone
  crystal beads
6 silver 12mm donut disks
  with holes
12 silver 6mm jump rings
Silver fold-over crimp

6 silver 1.5mm head pins
56" (142 cm) silver unsoldered
  elongated cable chain
57" (145 cm) purple faux
  suede cord
12½" (3.8 cm) green faux
  suede cord
Jeweler's cement

## ■ TOOLS

Round-nose pliers
Chain-nose pliers
Wire cutters
Scissors

## ■ FINISHED SIZE

56" (142 cm)

**Step 1.** Tie an overhand knot every 5" (12.5 cm) on the purple suede cord.

**Step 2.** Thread a jump ring through each knot.

**Step 3.** Attach 1 silver donut to every other jump ring.

**Step 4.** Pass the end of a head pin through 1 crystal and 1 lampworked bead.

**Step 5.** Make a wrapped loop above the lampworked bead.

**Step 6.** Repeat Steps 5–6 for all the beads.

**Step 7.** Attach a beaded head pin to every other knot on the purple suede cord.

**Step 8.** Overlap the ends of the purple suede cord inside the fold-over crimp.

**Step 9.** Place a drop of glue on the purple suede ends, then use chain nose pliers to close the fold-over crimp.

**Step 10.** Pass one end of the chain through the jump rings that are attached to the purple suede cord. Connect the ends of the chain.

**Step 11.** Cut the green suede cord into 12 lengths.

**Step 12.** Tie a piece of green suede cord over the fold-over crimp and adjacent chain.

**Step 13.** Hold the chain and purple suede cords together and tie lengths of green suede around them evenly spaced between purple knots.

## USING CHAIN

Jewelry makers have been incorporating chain into their designs for years because it adds a contemporary, upscale look. Chain is available in a variety of materials, including sterling silver and silver-plated. Use sterling for long-lasting pieces because it adds value and can be polished. Choose silver-plated chain for trendier designs because it's inexpensive and replaceable. Decide what your budget can handle and then go from there.

There are many different styles of chain. To choose the most appropriate one, think about the overall look of the design. Figaro chain is classic, curb is funky, elongated chain is contemporary, and very thin cable chain is understated and elegant. The same necklace made with each style of chain would look completely different!

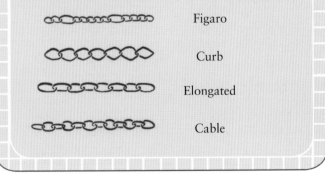

Figaro

Curb

Elongated

Cable

# NECKLACE

This organic necklace is a
contemporary twist on your
grandma's strand of knotted pearls.
You use the same technique, but
the beads and pendant give it a
completely different look.

*Use a traditional technique to make some modern magic.*

## ■ MATERIALS

45mm etched shell pendant
  with bail
6 blue quartz 6mm round
  beads
9 tiger's eye 6mm round beads
3 red aventurine 6mm round
  beads
3 red aventurine 6mm tubes
3 sodalite 8mm buttons
6 red aventurine 6mm chips
9 brown 6mm freshwater
  pearls
6 sodalite 6mm
  side-drilled ovals

3 red aventurine 10mm
  rectangles
3 sodalite 10mm rectangles
3 sodalite 6mm tubes
3 blue quartz 10mm ovals
3 carnelian chips
1/2" (1.3 cm) silver French wire
2m carded white silk
  with needle
Jeweler's cement
Silver duet clasp
2 silver 6mm jump rings

## ■ TOOLS

Chain-nose pliers
Beading awl or
  knotting tool
Scissors

## ■ FINISHED SIZE

11½" (29 cm)

**Step 1.** Separate the beads into groups of three similar beads each.
**Step 2.** Cut the length of French wire in half.
**Step 3.** Pass the needle through the French wire, three beads, and a jump ring.
**Step 4.** Follow the instructions for knotting between beads. (See page 61)
**Step 5.** Attach the pendant to the center of the finished necklace.

# KNOTTY HEMP BELT

Macramé is back in style! Square knots are easy to
master and can be combined to make jewelry and
other beaded accessories like cool chokers, fun pet
leashes, and this super stylish belt.

*... bell bottoms and sandals are optional ...*

**Step 1.** Hold all the cords together, leave 12" (30.5 cm) at the end,
and tie the cords in an overhand knot.

**Step 2.** Arrange the strands so there are six strands to one side.
Divide these strands into three groups of two strands.

**Step 3.** For each group of six strands, tie the outside strands around
the inside strands in a square knot.

**Step 4.** Bring the inside strands from each group of six strands to
the center.

**Step 5.** Use the middle strands from each group of six strands to tie
a square knot around the four strands in the center.

**Step 6.** Hold the four center strands together and pass them
through one 10mm bead. Tie another square knot.

**Step 7.** Repeat Steps 2–6 until the beaded section is complete.

**Step 8.** After the last set of square knots, tie the ends in an
overhand knot.

**Step 9.** String one 8mm bead 1–2" (2.5–5 cm) from each cord end
and pass the cord end back through the bead to hold it in place.

68

**MATERIALS**

Twelve 3-yd (2.74-m) lengths of 20# test (1.5mm) hemp cord

12 light brown and 12 dark brown 8mm wooden beads

23 light brown and 3 dark brown 10mm wooden beads

**TOOLS**

Scissors

**FINISHED SIZE**

Knotted section:
36" (91.5 cm)
Total length:
56" (142 cm)

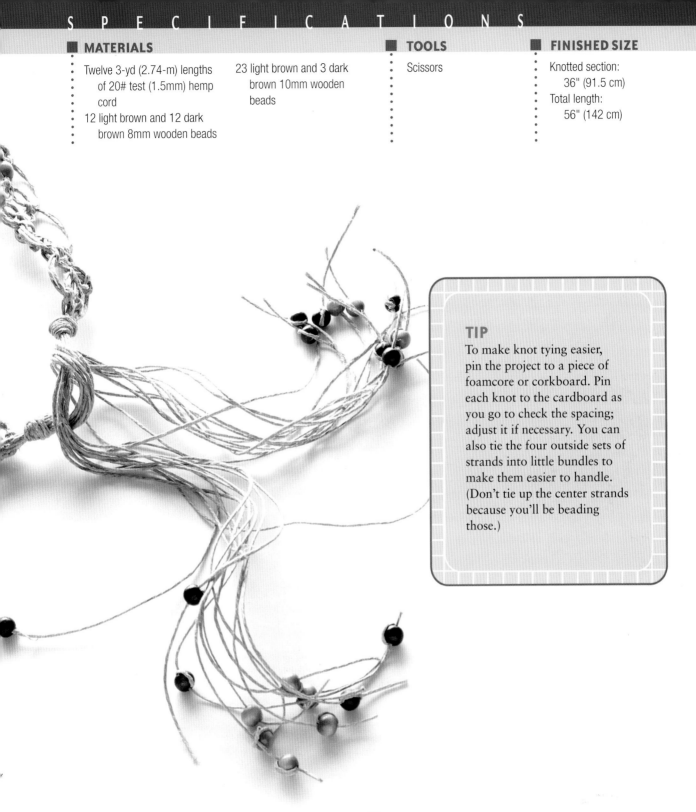

**TIP**

To make knot tying easier, pin the project to a piece of foamcore or corkboard. Pin each knot to the cardboard as you go to check the spacing; adjust it if necessary. You can also tie the four outside sets of strands into little bundles to make them easier to handle. (Don't tie up the center strands because you'll be beading those.)

## TYING SQUARE KNOTS

Square knots are the basic building blocks for most macramé projects. You can make them with or without center strands.

### ■ Basic square knot:

1. Bring the right strand over the left strand and through the loop to tie a half knot—the same knot you use to tie your shoe. See Figure 1.

2. Bring the left strand over the right strand and through the loop to tie another half knot. See Figure 2.

### ■ Square knot with center strands:

1. Bring the right strand over the center strands, then bring the left strand under the center strands and through the loop. See Figure 1.

2. Bring the left strand over the center strands, then bring the right strand under the center strands and through the loop. See Figure 2.

*Figure 1*

*Figure 1*

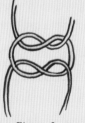

*Figure 2*

*Figure 2*

# RICH STITCHES

## STITCHING WITH BEADS

is a fun way to turn a plain and ordinary garment or object into a unique, personalized treasure. ■ You don't even have to know how to sew. ■ Pick up some needles and beading thread and get started. You'll be surprised by how easy it is!

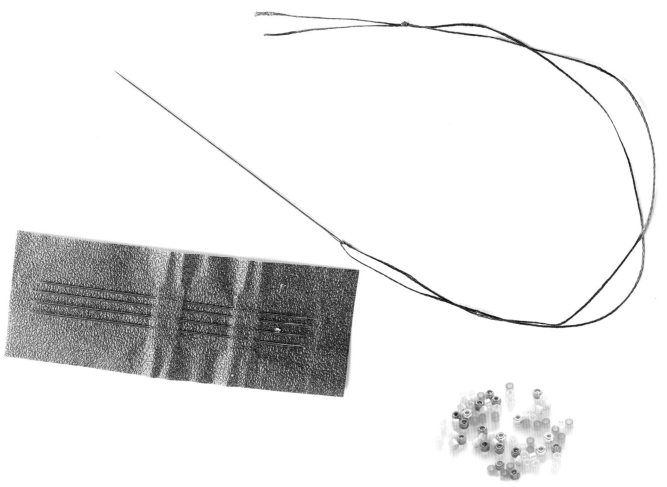

# TANK TOP

Add flair to a store-bought tank top with this easy stitching pattern. The project proves that you don't have to be a master with needle and thread to create fun wearable embellishments!

*Make it your own!*

## ■ MATERIALS

- 15 magenta 8mm square sequins
- 15 green 6mm round sequins
- 15 green 11° seed beads
- 18" (45.5 cm) of white beading thread
- Tank top

## ■ TOOLS

- Sharp beading needle
- Scissors
- Pencil

## ■ FINISHED SIZE

7" beaded row

**Step 1.** Measure 3½" (9 cm) to the left of center of the neckline and make a light pencil mark.

**Step 2.** Thread the needle and tie a knot in the thread end.

**Step 3.** Stitch through the tank-top edge from back to front on the pencil mark.

**Step 4.** Pass the needle through 1 square sequin, 1 round sequin, and 1 seed bead.

**Step 5.** Pass the needle back through the sequins and inside the hem. (See Figure 1.)

**Step 6.** Pass the needle to the front of the hem about ½" (1.3 cm) from the first beaded sequin.

**Step 7.** Repeat Steps 4–6 fourteen more times.

**Step 8.** Knot the thread on the back of the hem and cut off any extra thread.

*Figure 1*

■ VARIATION

You can use the same technique to add sequins and seed beads to almost anything, including this cool headband. Use round and square sequins to mix up the design a little.

# RETRO BEADED
# JOURNAL

Journals make great last-minute gifts. Customize a fun
fabric journal with a beaded strip of leather. You
can use this easy technique to decorate cards,
ribbon, clothing, and more!

*Jazz-up your journal with this easy technique.*

### ■ MATERIALS

Blue/aqua/brown 6 x 7"
(15 x 18 cm) fabric-covered
journal
1¹/₄ x 8" (3.2 x 20.5 cm) strip
of very thin tan leather
18 matte brown 10mm
bugle beads

3 aqua 8mm glass
flower beads
3 brown 11° seed beads
24" (61 cm) of white
beading thread
Fabric glue
Glue stick

### ■ TOOLS

Sharp beading needle
Scissors

### ■ FINISHED SIZE

6 x 7" (15 x 18 cm)

*Figure 1*

**Step 1.** Thread the needle and tie a knot at the end of the thread.

**Step 2.** Pass the needle through the center of the leather strip from back to front.

**Step 3.** Pass the needle through 1 aqua flower and 1 seed bead.

**Step 4.** Pass the needle back through the aqua flower.

**Step 5.** Pass the needle through the leather near a petal on the flower.

**Step 6.** Pass the needle through 1 bugle bead and back through the leather.

**Step 7.** Continue adding bugle beads evenly spaced around the flower as shown. See Figure 1.

**Step 8.** Measure 2" (5 cm) from the first flower and repeat Steps 3–7 above and below the center flower on the leather strip.

**Step 9.** Lay the leather strip across the front of the journal with ¹/₂" (1.3 cm) extending over the upper and lower edges.

**Step 10.** Open the journal and use fabric glue to adhere the ends of the leather strip inside the front cover of the journal.

**Step 11.** Use a glue stick to glue the first page of the journal to the inside of the front cover to conceal the leather strip ends.

*. . . a touch of flower power . . .*

## ALOHA FLOWER
# FRAME

Personalize a picture frame with a bright splash of beaded color. This flower is so hip that you'll want to make several. Wear one as a brooch, turn one into a magnet, or stitch one on a purse.

**Step 1.** Trace and transfer the patterns onto the pieces of felt. See Figure 1 and Figure 2.

**Step 2.** Cut out the flower pieces and leaves.

**Step 3.** Thread the needle and knot the end.

**Step 4.** Starting between petals, stitch red beads to the edges of the orange flower. Backstitch through every second or third bead or as necessary to hold the beads in place.

**Step 5.** After you've stitched all the red beads, knot the thread but don't remove the needle.

**Step 6.** Layer the magenta flower on top of the orange flower.

## ■ MATERIALS

Felt squares: 2½" (6.5 cm)
orange, 2" (5 cm) magenta,
2" (5 cm) teal
Multicolor 10mm millefiori
disk bead
10mm bugle beads: 5 clear,
6 aqua
2 clear iridescent
5mm round sequins
80 red iridescent
11° seed beads

36" (91.5 cm) of white
beading thread
Fabric glue
Industrial-strength glue
Dark brown 3" (7.5 cm)
distressed wooden
picture frame
Tracing and transfer paper

## ■ TOOLS

Pencil
Sharp beading needle
Scissors

## ■ FINISHED SIZE

Flower: 3½" (9 cm)

**Step 7.** Stitch the millefiori bead in place on the magenta flower to hold the two flowers together.

**Step 8.** Stitch 1 clear bugle bead to each petal of the magenta flower.

**Step 9.** Knot the thread on the back of the orange flower and cut off any extra thread.

**Step 10.** Glue the leaves to the flower as shown.

**Step 11.** Thread the needle and use it to stitch 3 bugle beads fanning out from the center of a leaf.

**Step 12.** Pass the needle through 1 sequin and 1 seed bead on the leaf tip, then knot the thread and cut off any extra.

**Step 13.** Repeat Steps 11–12 to embellish the other leaf.

**Step 14.** Use industrial-strength glue to attach the flower to the lower left corner of a picture frame.

### BACKSTITCH WITH BEADS

A simple way to keep beads in place is by backstitching. String 4 beads. Hold them in place against the fabric. Pass the needle through the fabric after the last bead. Pass up through the fabric between the second and third beads and pass through the last 2 beads strung. Continue by adding more beads and backstitching as necessary to hold them in place.

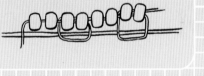

*Figure 1*

*Figure 2*

# FUNKY FELTED
# PURSE

Beaded blanket stitch adds a fun, whimsical touch to almost anything. Use long bugle beads to make the stitches uniform. Mix bright colors that coordinate with your bag, or use mono-chromatic tones for a subtle look.

**Step 1.** Follow the instructions for Blanket Stitch with Beads.

**Step 2.** Make eight blanket stitches along the outer edge of the flap.

**Step 3.** Pass the needle through 3 beads to encircle the corner, then backstitch as necessary to hold them in place.

**Step 4.** Sew blanket stitches across the lower edge of the flap.

**Step 5.** Repeat Step 3 and 2.

**Step 6.** To finish the stitches, pass the needle through the last stitch again and tie a knot to hold it in place.

**Step 7.** Stitch 1 crystal bead to the center of the flap.

**Step 8.** Stitch millefiori beads in a diamond pattern fanning out from the crystal bead.

**Step 9.** Cut a piece of felt to cover the inside of the flap.

**Step 10.** Spread glue on the felt, then press it to the inside of the flap to cover the stitches and thread ends.

## BLANKET STITCH WITH BEADS

1. Place 2 bugle beads end to end and measure them.
2. Bring the needle up through the fabric at that distance from the fabric edge.
3. Pass the needle through 2 bugle beads, then take the needle to the back of the flap and bring the needle up at the same point as in Step 2, leaving the beads on the front side.
4. Pass the needle through the beads.
5. Knot the thread end to the first stitch.
6. Pass the needle through 3 bugle beads and through the fabric at the 2-bead measurement from the edge.
7. Bring the needle under the thread between the first and second beads, then make the next stitch.

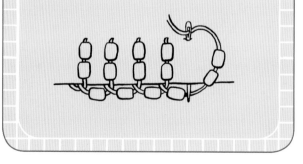

## MATERIALS

- 9 x 8" (23 x 20.5 cm) felted purse with 7½ x 4" (18.5 x 10 cm) flap
- 4 blue/red 15mm square millefiori glass beads
- Siam 8mm faceted round crystal bead
- 93 size 10mm bugle beads: red, blue, aqua
- 108" (274.3 cm) white beading thread
- 7 x 3" (18 x 7.5 cm) piece of blue felt
- Fabric glue

## TOOLS

- Sharp beading needle
- Scissors

## FINISHED SIZE

- 9 x 8" (23 x 20.5 cm)

*Add some color with an easy beaded border.*

79

# WOVEN
# WONDERS

**THERE ARE MANY DIFFERENT STYLES** of bead weaving, from simple ladder stitch to intricate peyote stitch. ■ These projects are a sampler platter, meant to give you just a taste of a few different styles. ■ Bon appétit!

## BEJEWELED CRYSTAL
# BRACELET

This lacy bracelet is a good introduction to bead weaving because large beads make it easy and the end result is so impressive! Use silver beading wire to add metallic shine and intensify the bracelet shape.

## ■ MATERIALS

- 26 tanzanite 12x5mm crystal briolettes
- 52 peridot 4mm faceted round crystal beads
- 42 Pacific opal 6mm faceted round crystal beads
- 48" (122 cm) length of .018" diameter silver 49-strand beading wire
- 6 silver crimp tubes
- 2 silver 3-to-1 end connectors
- 2 silver 5mm split rings
- Silver lobster clasp
- Silver extension chain
- Silver head pin

## ■ TOOLS

- Round-nose pliers
- Chain-nose pliers
- Wire cutters
- Crimping tool

## ■ FINISHED SIZE

- 6–8" (15–20.5 cm) adjustable

**Step 1.** Cut four 12" (30.5 cm) lengths of silver beading wire.

**Step 2.** Use a crimp tube to attach one end of a wire to each outer loop on a ring end connector. Hold two wires together and attach them to the center loop. (see page 59)

**Step 3.** Separate the strands into two sets, each with one outer strand and one center strand.

**Step 4.** Using one set of strands, pass an outer wire through 1 Pacific opal bead. Pass a center wire through the opposite end of the same bead.

**Step 5.** Pass the center wire through 1 Pacific opal bead.

**Step 6.** Pass an outer wire through 1 peridot bead, 1 briolette, and 1 peridot bead.

**Step 7.** Pass a center wire through 1 Pacific opal bead. Pass the outer wire through the opposite end of the same Pacific opal bead to form a circle.

**Step 8.** Repeat Steps 4–7 using the other set of wires and connecting the circles by passing the center wire through the existing Pacific opal bead in Step 5. To make consistent stitches, adjust the wire tension as you go. See Figure 1.

**Step 9.** Repeat the beading pattern twelve more times to make a beaded section that is about 5½" (14 cm) long.

**Step 10.** Use crimp tubes to attach the beading wires to an end connector as in Step 2.

**Step 11.** Use a split ring to attach a clasp to one end of the bracelet and an extension chain to the other end.

**Step 12.** String 1 Pacific opal bead on a head pin. Make a wrapped loop to attach it to the end of the extension chain. (see page 47)

*Figure 1*

## ■ VARIATION

Use the same technique to customize home décor. To add texture and interest to the beaded design, this candleholder features smooth dark blue beads contrasted with fire-polished aqua beads in the center of the stitches.

# OCEANSIDE BLING
# NECKLACE

These big, glittery beads call for special treatment. Use right-angle weave to create a few intricately beaded beads to add to the mix. Just a touch of bead weaving adds so much to what would otherwise be a simple stringing project.

## ■ BEADED BEADS

**Step 1.** Use wire cutters to cut the beading wire in three equal lengths.

**Step 2.** String 4 beads about 2" (5 cm) from the end of one length of beading wire.

**Step 3.** Place a small piece of adhesive tape over the short end of the wire to hold the beads in place.

**Step 4.** Pass the long wire end through the first bead to complete one right-angle-weave stitch.

**Step 5.** Make five more right-angle-weave stitches.

**Step 6.** Step up to the next row and complete six right-angle-weave stitches.

**Step 7.** Weave the wire ends through the beads to connect the two ends of the woven piece to form a tube shape.

**Step 8.** Tie the ends together in a square knot. (see page 70) Place a drop of glue on the knot, let it dry, and cut off any extra wire.

## ■ MATERIALS

### BEADED BEADS

90 Pacific opal 4mm faceted round crystal beads
42" (106.5 cm) length of .010" beading wire
Jeweler's cement
Adhesive tape

### NECKLACE

8 peridot 4mm faceted round crystal beads
Clear AB 10mm crystal beads: 4 round, 4 cube
10mm rectangular dichroic glass beads: 2 teal, 2 peridot
13mm twist dichroic glass beads: 2 teal, 2 peridot
4 clear 14mm round dichroic glass beads
2 clear 10mm twist dichroic glass beads
4 clear 13mm rhomboid dichroic glass beads
2 green 10mm rolled dichroic glass beads
4 aqua 12mm round dichroic glass beads
Green 7mm round dicrhoic glass bead
3 aqua 12mm dichroic glass washers
4 clear/olive 12mm borosilicate glass washers
35mm pewter donut pendant
Sterling silver 2mm crimp tube
2 sterling silver crimp ends
2 sterling silver 6mm split rings
Sterling silver square toggle clasp
20" (51 cm) length of .024" beading wire

## ■ TOOLS

Wire cutters
Crimping tool

## ■ FINISHED SIZE

23" (58.5 cm)

## ■ NECKLACE

**Step 1.** String 8 peridot crystals onto the center of the beading wire.

**Step 2.** Place the pewter donut over the crystal beads.

**Step 3.** Hold the wire ends together and pass them through a crimp tube. Crimp it. (see page 28)

**Step 4.** Hold the wire ends together and string beads as follows: 1 aqua washer, one 14mm round clear, 1 beaded bead, one 14mm round clear, one 8mm green.

**Step 5.** Separate the strands.

**Step 6.** String the following beads onto one strand: one 10mm clear twist, one 12mm round aqua, one 12mm round crystal, 1 beaded bead, one 14mm round clear.

**Step 7.** Arrange half the remaining beads on the strand as desired.

**Step 8.** Attach a crimp end to the end of the beading wire.

**Step 9.** Use a split ring to attach the crimp end to half of the clasp.

**Step 10.** Repeat Steps 6–9 so the necklace is symmetrical.

### RIGHT-ANGLE WEAVE

1. String 4 beads and pass through them again to make the first stitch.
2. For the next stitch, string 3 beads and pass through the last bead from the first stitch and through the first 2 just strung.
3. To step up to the next row, pass through the last 3 beads strung to exit through the side of the last stitch.
4. String 3 beads, pass through the last bead passed through, and pass through the stitch to exit the top bead.
5. Continue adding stitches. To tie off the ends, weave through the end beads until the thread exits adjacent beads.

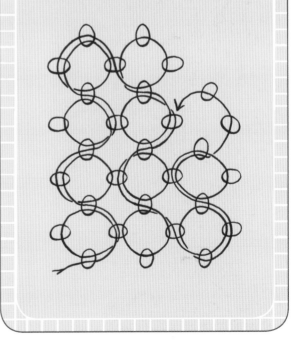

CREATIVE CAUSE

# BRACELET

Are you wearing your cause on your sleeve? Make yours stand out from the crowd with these cool peyote bands. A bit of space between the bands means that the bracelet remains flexible but oh so stylish.

## ■ MATERIALS

- Cylinder seed beads: metallic blue, yellow, green, purple
- 2yd (1.82 m) white beading thread
- Cause bracelet
- Jeweler's cement
- Adhesive tape

## ■ TOOLS

- Sharp beading needle
- Scissors

## ■ FINISHED SIZE

- ³/₄" (one beaded band)

## ■ INSTRUCTIONS FOR ONE BEADED BAND

**Step 1.** Pass the needle through enough beads to fit around the bracelet (22 beads for Livestrong bracelet).

**Step 2.** Follow the tubular peyote instructions to make two rows of blue beads.

**Step 3.** Adjust the beaded band so the step-up is close to the inside edge of the bracelet.

**Step 4.** Turn the bracelet inside out to facilitate stepping up to the next row.

**Step 5.** Start a new color when you step up. Add three rows of purple, two to three rows of yellow, three rows of green, and two rows of blue.

**Step 6.** Pass the needle back through the stitches on the inside of the bracelet so the ends are exiting through adjoining beads.

**Step 7.** Tie the ends in a square knot and place a drop of glue on the knot. (see page 70)

**Step 8.** Let the glue dry, then carefully cut off the extra thread.

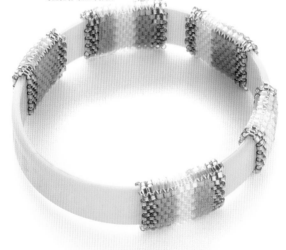

## TUBULAR PEYOTE STITCH

These instructions are for even-count tubular peyote stitch. Odd-count is the same except you don't have to step up at the end of the row, the pattern just keeps spiraling around.

1. Place a piece of adhesive tape about 2" (5 cm) from the end of the thread.
2. Pass the needle through the number of beads it takes to encircle the surface.
3. Pull the ends in a snug circle and tie them in a square knot. See Figure 1.
4. Place a drop of jeweler's cement on the knot and remove the adhesive tape.
5. Pass the needle through the first bead next to the knot.
6. Add a bead and pass the needle through the third bead. See Figure 2.
7. Continue to add a bead/skip a bead until you reach the end of the row. Use your thumbnail to press beads into place as you continue adding to the row.
8. To step up to the next row, pass the needle through the last bead from the previous row and the first bead added for the new row.

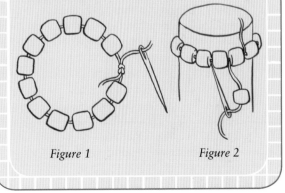

*Figure 1*                    *Figure 2*

# RIGHTEOUS
## RIGHT-ANGLE WEAVE
# BRACELET

Perfect your right-angle technique with this gorgeous woven bracelet. The matte cube beads and sparkly crystals are the perfect combination for a design that combines simplicity with opulence.

*Mix shiny and matte beads for an eclectic, designer look.*

**Step 1.** Use chain-nose pliers to open the jump rings. Connect one jump ring to the round part of the toggle clasp and use one jump ring to connect the 1/2" (1.3 cm) length of chain to the toggle bar. Set them aside.

**Step 2.** Thread the needle and use cube beads to make seventeen right-angle weave stitches in the first row. See page 85.

**Step 3.** Step up to the second row and make seventeen right-angle-weave stitches back to the beginning of the bracelet.

**Step 4.** Pass the needle through three 11° beads, one 6° bead, half of the clasp, one 6° bead, and three 11° beads.

**Step 5.** Pass the needle through one 6° bead, 1 crystal, and one 11° bead.

**Step 6.** Pass the needle back through the crystal and 6° bead and the first vertical row of cube beads.

### ■ MATERIALS

122 maroon/indigo
    4mm cube beads
36 fuchsia 4mm faceted
    round crystal beads
40 matte gray 6° seed beads
48 pewter 11° seed beads

Silver toggle clasp with
    fuchsia crystals
2 silver 6mm oval jump rings
1/2" (1.3 cm) of silver curb chain
4yd (3.65 m) of black thread
Jeweler's cement

### ■ TOOLS

Chain-nose pliers
Sharp beading needle
Scissors

### ■ FINISHED SIZE

7" (18 cm)

**Step 7.** Repeat Steps 5–6 to add one 6° bead, 1 crystal, and one 11° seed bead to the other side of the bracelet. See Figure 1.

**Step 8.** Pass through the beads that attach to the clasp several times to make the clasp extra strong.

**Step 9.** To get to the next vertical row, pass the needle through the nearest stitch and continue adding the crystal edging to the bracelet.

**Step 10.** Repeat Step 5 to attach the clasp to the other end of the bracelet. Pass through the beads that attach to the clasp several times to make the clasp extra strong.

**Step 11.** Weave back through the bracelet to strengthen it and make the thread ends exit from adjoining beads. Tie the ends in a knot.

**Step 12.** Place a drop of glue on the knot, let it dry, and carefully cut off any extra thread with scissors.

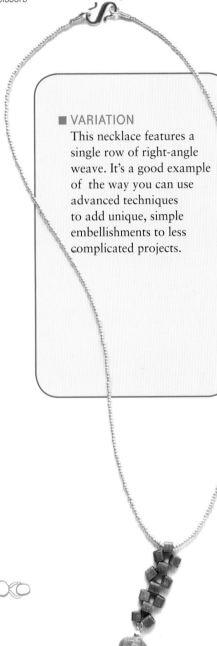

### ■ VARIATION

This necklace features a single row of right-angle weave. It's a good example of the way you can use advanced techniques to add unique, simple embellishments to less complicated projects.

*Figure 1*

89

# SUPPLIERS

Check with your local bead shop or contact these suppliers.

Beadalon
(866) 4-BEADALON
www.beadalon.com
(Beading wire and general beading supplies)

Blue Moon Beads
www.bluemoonbeads.com
(Specialty beads and findings)

Charm Factory, Inc.
PO Box 91625
Albuquerque, NM 87199
(866) 867-5266
www.charmfactory.com
(Sterling silver charms and bracelets)

Fire Mountain Gems and Beads
One Fire Mountain Wy.
Grants Pass, OR 97526
(800) 355-2137
www.firemountaingems.com
(General beading supplies)

Green Girl Studios
49 Reynolda Dr.
Asheville, NC 28803
(828) 298-2263
www.greengirlstudios.com
(Cast pewter beads)

Halcraft USA, Inc.
(212) 376-1580
www.halcraft.com
(General beading supplies)

JHB International
(303) 751-8100
www.buttons.com
(Buttons)

Kristal Wick Creations
6110 Dudley St.
Arvada, CO 80004
(866) 811-1376
www.KristalWick.com
(Handpainted silk beads)

Lillypilly Designs
PO Box 270136
Louisville, CO 80027
(303) 543-8673
www.lillypillydesigns.com
(Etched shell pendants and beads)

Nancy Tobey Glass Beads
76 Pleasant St.
Ayer, MA 01432
(978) 772-3317
www.nancytobey.com
(Borosilicate glass beads)

National Cancer Society
www.cancersocietystore.com
(Livestrong and Hope bracelets)

Paula Radke Dichroic Glass Beads
(800) 341-4945
www.paularadke.com
(Dichroic glass beads and components)

Pure Allure
(800) 536-6312
www.pureallure.com
(Metal components featuring
   Swarovski crystal)

Rio Grande
7500 Bluewater Rd. NW
Albuquerque, NM 87121
(800) 545-6566
www.riogrande.com
(General beading supplies)

Soft Flex Company
PO Box 80
Sonoma, CA 95476
(707) 938-3539
www.softflexcompany.com

Swarovski North America, Ltd.
www.create-your-style.com
(Austrian crystals and components)

Thunderbird Supply Company
1907 W. Historic Rte. 66
Gallup, NM 87301
(800) 545-7968
www.thunderbirdsupply.com
(General beading supplies)

Toho Co, Ltd.
www.tohobeads.net
(Japanese seed beads)

# INDEX

**a**wls 9

**b**ackstitch 77
barrettes, Sparkly Beaded 48–49
bead boards 8
bead links, making 59
beads 3–4, 29, 31, 34, 48, 55, 56, 73; crimp 5
belt, Knotty Hemp 68–69
blanket stitch 78
bracelet lengths 37
bracelets
    Antique Button 12–13
    Bejeweled Crystal 82–83
    Cha-Cha 54–55
    Creative Cause 86–87
    Fit-for-a-Queen 32–33
    Found Object Charm 16–17
    Great Lengths 35–36
    Righteous Right-Angle Weave 88–89
    Rock 'N Roll Cuff 50–51
buttons 13

**c**andle, Clever Wrap 57–58; variation 83
chain 5, 65
charms 17, 25
clasps 5, 6
color combinations 21
connectors 5, 6; making bead 59
cords 7
crimping tool 9
crimps 5; attaching to clasps 28
cutters, wire 9

**d**esigns, pattern 41

**e**arrings
    Glamour Girl 56–57
    Quick and Easy 46–47
ear wires 5
eye pins 5

**f**indings 5–6, earring 56
frame, Aloha Flower 76–77

**g**lass beads 34
glue 15

**h**ead pins 6
hill tribe silver 53

**j**ournal, Retro Beaded 74–75
jump rings 6

**k**notting 61, 69; square 70

**l**oops, making wire 47

**m**easurements 37
memory wire 7, 22, 23

**n**ecklace lengths 37
necklaces
    Center Stage Opera 64–65
    Chunky Nugget 20–21
    Double Trouble Choker 22–23
    Follow Your Heart Faux Lariat 24–25
    Great Lengths 35–36
    Illusion-style 40
    Knock-Out Knotted 66–67
    Lucious Lariat 38–39
    Mod Millefiori 58–59
    Oceanside Bling 84–85
    Twice as Nice 26–27
    World Beat Choker 62–63
    Y Not 52–53
needles 8

**p**liers 9
projects
purse
    Funky Felted 78–79
    In Vogue 42–43

**r**eamers 9
resources 90
right-angle weave 85

**S**-hooks 6
scrapbook, Stylish 14–15
sequins 73
split rings 6
silver, hill tribe 54; sterling 54
stitches, backstitch 77; blanket 78; right-angle
    weave 85; tubular peyote 87
stitching beads 72–79
supplies 3–9
stringing material 7–8

**t**ank top, Trendy 72–78
thread, stringing 7–8
    techniques
        attaching crimps to clasps 28
        backstitch with beads 77
        blanket stitch with beads 78
        knots, tying 70
        knotting between beads 61
        making bead links 59
        making wire loops 47
        right-angle weave 85
        tubular peyote stitch 87
        tying square knots 70
    tips
        all about art glass 34
        charm bracelet 17
        choosing right adhesive 15
        color combinations 21
        common beading patterns 41
        hill tribe silver 53
        knotting 61
        making watches 31
        personalizing designs 25
        standard jewelry lengths 37
        using chain 65
        working with memory wire 23
tools 8–9
tubing, rubber 22
tubular peyote stitch 87

**w**atch, Time to Bead 30–31
wire 6, 7, 22, 23
wire cutters 9
wire loops, making 47